Education at a Glance 2014

HIGHLIGHTS

OECD
BETTER POLICIES FOR BETTER LIVES

This work is published under the responsibility of the Secretary-General of the OECD. The opinions expressed and arguments employed herein do not necessarily reflect the official views of OECD member countries.

This document and any map included herein are without prejudice to the status of or sovereignty over any territory, to the delimitation of international frontiers and boundaries and to the name of any territory, city or area.

Please cite this publication as:
OECD (2014), *Education at a Glance 2014: Highlights*, OECD Publishing.
http://dx.doi.org/10.1787/eag_highlights-2014-en

ISBN 978-92-64-21501-6 (print)
ISBN 978-92-64-21502-3 (PDF)
ISBN 978-92-64-21875-8 (HTML)

Education at a Glance
ISSN 2076-2631 (print)
ISSN 2076-264X (online)

The statistical data for Israel are supplied by and under the responsibility of the relevant Israeli authorities. The use of such data by the OECD is without prejudice to the status of the Golan Heights, East Jerusalem and Israeli settlements in the West Bank under the terms of international law.

Photo credits: Cover © Blue Jean images/Getty images.
Images: Chapter 1 © Jeffrey Coolidge/The Image Bank/Getty Images.
          Chapter 2 ©Wavebreakmedia /Shutterstock.
          Chapter 3 © Tom Grill/Photographer's Choice RF/Getty Images.
          Chapter 4 © Julia Smith/Riser/Getty Images.
          Chapter 5 © Image Source/Getty Images.
          Chapter 6 © Andrey_Popov /Shutterstock.com.

Corrigenda to OECD publications may be found on line at: *www.oecd.org/about/publishing/corrigenda.htm.*

Foreword

Education at a Glance 2014: Highlights *offers a reader-friendly introduction to the OECD's collection of internationally comparable data on education.*

As the name suggests, it is derived from Education at a Glance 2014, *the OECD's flagship compendium of education statistics. However, it differs from that publication in a number of ways, most significantly in its structure, which is made up of six sections that explore the following topics:*

- **Education levels and student numbers:** *This section looks at education levels and trends in the general population, early childhood and secondary education systems.*

- **Higher education and work:** *This section looks at how many students enter and successfully complete tertiary education, as well as young people's transition from school to the world of work.*

- **The economic and social benefits of education:** *This section looks at the extent to which education brings economic gains to individuals, in the form of higher incomes and lower unemployment rates, and at how these benefits serve as an incentive for people and societies to invest in education. It also examines the societal benefits related to having a highly educated population.*

- **Paying for education:** *This section looks at how much countries spend on education, the role of private spending, what education money is spent on and whether countries are getting value for money.*

- **The school environment:** *This section looks at how much time teachers spend at work, how much of that time is spent teaching, class sizes, and teachers and their salaries.*

- **Skills for life:** *This special section looks at why skills are so important, how do education and socio-economic background affect them, and what is the role of adult learning.*

In general, this publication uses the terminology employed in Education at a Glance 2014. *However, in one or two places terminology has been simplified. Readers who want to find out more should consult the Reader's guide.*

Tables and charts in this volume are accompanied by a dynamic hyperlink, or StatLink, that will direct readers to an Internet site where the corresponding data are available in Excel™ format. In addition, reference is sometimes made in the text to charts and tables that appear in Education at a Glance 2014. *This material can generally be accessed via the StatLinks accompanying the tables and charts in the relevant indicator, or at www.oecd.org/edu/eag.htm.*

Readers wishing to find out more about the OECD's work on education should go to www.oecd.org/edu.

Table of contents

Follow OECD Publications on:

 http://twitter.com/OECD_Pubs

 http://www.facebook.com/OECDPublications

 http://www.linkedin.com/groups/OECD-Publications-4645871

 http://www.youtube.com/oecdilibrary

 http://www.oecd.org/oecddirect/

This book has...

A service that delivers Excel® files from the printed page!

Look for the *StatLinks* at the bottom of the tables or graphs in this book. To download the matching Excel® spreadsheet, just type the link into your Internet browser, starting with the *http://dx.doi.org* prefix, or click on the link from the e-book edition.

Executive summary: The benefits of expanded access to education are not shared equitably

Access to education continues to expand and the proportion of adults who are highly skilled in literacy, continues to grow; but socio-economic divisions are deepening, because the impact of education and skills on individuals' life chances has strengthened considerably.

The labour market rewards high educational attainment and high skills

Take the employment situation. On average, over 80% of tertiary-educated adults are employed compared to less than 60% of people with below upper secondary education. Yet tertiary-educated people, especially young adults, are not immune to unemployment. On average across OECD countries, the unemployment rate among tertiary-educated adults stood at 5.0% in 2012 (up from 3.3% in 2008), but among 25-34 year-olds, it was 7.4% (up from 4.6% in 2008). By comparison, the unemployment rate for 25-34 year-olds without an upper secondary education reached 19.8% in 2012 (and even higher in many countries), up from 13.6% in 2008. These data reconfirm that the recent economic crisis hit young, low-educated adults hardest.

A lack of skills only strengthens the risk of unemployment – even among people with similar levels of education. For example, on average across the 24 countries and sub-national regions that participated in the Survey of Adult Skills, 5.8% of adults without upper secondary education, but who had a moderate level of literacy proficiency, were unemployed in 2012 compared to 8.0% of adults with similar educational attainment but who had low levels of literacy proficiency. Similarly, among tertiary-educated adults, 3.9% of those with lower literacy proficiency were unemployed compared with 2.5% of those with the highest proficiency.

Data on earnings also point to a widening gap between the educational "haves" and "have-nots". Across OECD countries, adults with a tertiary degree earn about 70% more, on average, than those with upper secondary education. Differences in skills also have an impact on earnings, even among people with the same level of education: on average, a tertiary-educated adult who performs at the highest level of literacy proficiency earns about 45% more than a similarly educated adult who performs at the lowest level in literacy, as measured by the Survey of Adult Skills.

In most countries, absolute upward mobility in education is more common than downward mobility

The expansion of education systems in many OECD countries, both at the upper secondary or post-secondary non-tertiary and tertiary levels of education, has given 25-34 year-olds an opportunity to attain a higher level of education than their parents. On average across the OECD countries that participated in the 2012 Survey of Adult Skills (a product of the OECD Programme for the International Assessment of Adult Competencies, or PIAAC), 32% of young people have achieved a higher level of education than their parents, while only 16% have not attained their parents' education level. In all countries except Estonia, Germany, Norway and Sweden, absolute upward mobility in education is more common than absolute downward mobility. The expansion of education has been particularly pronounced in France, Ireland, Italy, Korea, Spain and the Russian Federation, where the difference between upward and downward educational mobility is 30 percentage points or more.

Other findings

- Close to 40% of 25-34 year-olds now have a tertiary education, a proportion 15 percentage points larger than that among 55-64 year-olds.

- There is a 10 percentage-point increase, on average, between the share of older and younger adults scoring at the highest levels of literacy proficiency.

- In a majority of OECD countries, education now begins for most children well before they are 5 years old. More than three-quarters of 4-year-olds (84%) are enrolled in early childhood and primary education across OECD countries; among OECD countries that are part of the European Union, 89% of 4-year-olds are.

- Some 72% of students who begin upper secondary education complete the programmes they entered within the theoretical duration of the programme. Giving two extra years to students to complete their upper secondary programmes, 87% of students successfully complete programmes two years after the stipulated time of graduation, on average across OECD countries.

- On average across OECD countries in 2012, 49% of 15-29 year-olds were in education. Of the remaining 51%, 36% held a job, 7% were unemployed, and 8% were outside of the labour force.

- Tertiary institutions and, to a lesser extent, pre-primary institutions obtain the largest proportions of funds from private sources: 31% and 19%, respectively. Public funding on educational institutions, for all levels combined, increased between 2000 and 2011 in all countries (except Italy) for which comparable data are available. However, with more households sharing the cost of education, private funding increased at an even greater rate in more than three-quarters of countries.

- While the proportion of public expenditure devoted to education shrank in two-thirds of countries between 2005 and 2011, during the shorter period 2008-11 – the height of the economic crisis – public expenditure on education grew at a faster rate (or decreased at a slower rate) than public expenditure on all other services in 16 out of the 31 countries with available data.

- A master's degree is required of pre-primary school teachers in only four of the 35 countries with available data, while it is required of upper secondary teachers, who teach general subjects, in 22 of the 36 countries with available data.

- Professional development for teachers is compulsory at every level of education in about three-quarters of OECD and partner countries with available data. While it is required of all lower secondary teachers in 17 countries and for promotion or salary increase in 8 countries, it is not required in 6 countries.

- In 2012, more than 4.5 million students were enrolled in tertiary education outside their country of citizenship. Australia, Austria, Luxembourg, New Zealand, Switzerland and the United Kingdom have the highest proportion of international students as a percentage of their total tertiary enrolments.

Reader's guide

This section introduces some of the terminology used in this publication, and explains how readers can use the links provided to get further information.

Levels of education

Education systems vary considerably from country to country, including the ages at which students typically begin and end each phase of schooling, the duration of courses, and what students are taught and expected to learn. These variations greatly complicate the compilation of internationally comparable statistics on education. In response, the United Nations created an International Standard Classification of Education (ISCED), which provides a basis for comparing different education systems and a standard terminology.

The table below introduces this system of classification and explains what is meant by each level of education. Readers should note that this publication uses slightly simplified terminology, which differs from that used in both the ISCED classification and in *Education at a Glance 2014*. The table shows the equivalent terms in the two publications, the ISCED classifications and definitions of what it all means.

Term used to describe levels of education in *Education at a Glance 2014* *ISCED classification (and subcategories)*	Term generally used in this publication
Pre-primary education *ISCED 0*	**Pre-primary education** The first stage of organised instruction designed to introduce very young children to the school atmosphere. Minimum entry age of 3.
Primary education *ISCED 1*	**Primary education** Designed to provide a sound basic education in reading, writing and mathematics and a basic understanding of some other subjects. Entry age: between 5 and 7. Duration: 6 years.
Lower secondary education *ISCED 2 (subcategories: 2A prepares students for continuing academic education, leading to 3A; 2B has stronger vocational focus, leading to 3B; 2C offers preparation for entering workforce)*	**Lower secondary education** Completes provision of basic education, usually in a more subject-oriented way with more specialist teachers. Entry follows 6 years of primary education; duration is 3 years. In some countries, the end of this level marks the end of compulsory education.
Upper secondary education *ISCED 3 (subcategories: 3A prepares students for university-level education at level 5A ; 3B for entry into vocationally oriented tertiary education at level 5B; 3C prepares students for workforce or for post-secondary non tertiary education, ISCED 4)*	**Upper secondary education** Stronger subject specialisation than at lower-secondary level, with teachers usually more qualified. Students typically expected to have completed 9 years of education or lower secondary schooling before entry and are generally around the age of 15 or 16.
Post-secondary non-tertiary education *ISCED 4 (subcategories: 4A may prepare students for entry into tertiary education, both university level and vocationally oriented education; 4B typically prepares students to enter the workforce)*	**Post-secondary non-tertiary education** Programmes at this level may be regarded nationally as part of upper secondary or post-secondary education, but in terms of international comparison their status is less clear cut. Programme content may not be much more advanced than in upper secondary, and is certainly lower than at tertiary level. Entry typically requires completion of an upper secondary programme. Duration usually equivalent to between 6 months and 2 years of full-time study.

Term used to describe levels of education in *Education at a Glance 2014* *ISCED classification (and subcategories)*	Term generally used in this publication
Tertiary education *ISCED 5 (subcategories 5A and 5B, see below)*	**Tertiary education** ISCED 5 is the first stage of tertiary education (the second - ISCED 6 - involves advanced research). At level 5, it is often more useful to distinguish between two subcategories: 5A, which represent longer and more theoretical programmes; and 5B, where programmes are shorter and more practically oriented. Note, though, that as tertiary education differs greatly between countries, the demarcation between these two subcategories is not always clear cut.
Tertiary-type A education *ISCED 5A*	**University-level education** "Long-stream" programmes that are theory based and aimed at preparing students for further research or to give access to highly skilled professions, such as medicine or architecture. Entry preceded by 13 years of education, students typically required to have completed upper secondary or post-secondary non-tertiary education. Duration equivalent to at least 3 years of full-time study, but 4 is more usual.
Tertiary-type B education *ISCED 5B*	**Vocationally-oriented tertiary education** "Short-stream" programmes that are more practically oriented or focus on the skills needed for students to directly enter specific occupations. Entry preceded by 13 years of education; students may require mastery of specific subjects studied at levels 3B or 4A. Duration equivalent to at least 2 years of full-time study, but 3 is more usual.
Advanced research programmes *ISCED 6*	**Advanced research programmes** The second stage of tertiary education. Programmes are devoted to advanced study and original research.

For fuller definitions and explanations of the ISCED standard, please consult *Classifying Education Programmes: Manual for ISCED-97 Implementation in OECD Countries* (1999).

Country coverage

OECD and partner countries: This publication features data on education from the 34 OECD member countries, two partner countries that participate in the OECD Indicators of Education Systems Programme (INES), namely Brazil and the Russian Federation, and the other G20 countries that do not participate in INES (Argentina, China, Colombia, India, Indonesia, Latvia, Saudi Arabia and South Africa).

Belgium: Data on Belgium may be applicable only to either the Flemish Community or the French Community. Where this is the case, the text and charts refer to Belgium (Fl.) for the Flemish Community and Belgium (Fr.) for the French community.

EU21: These are the 21 OECD countries for which data are available or can be estimated that are members of the European Union: Austria, Belgium, the Czech Republic, Denmark, Estonia, Finland, France, Germany, Greece, Hungary, Ireland, Italy, Luxembourg, the Netherlands, Poland, Portugal, the Slovak Republic, Slovenia, Spain, Sweden and the United Kingdom.

G20: These are Argentina, Australia, Brazil, Canada, China, France, Germany, India, Indonesia, Italy, Japan, Korea, Mexico, the Russian Federation, Saudi Arabia, South Africa, Turkey, the United Kingdom, the United States and the European Union (which is not included in the G20 average).

Israel: The statistical data for Israel are supplied by and under the responsibility of the relevant Israeli authorities. The use of such data by the OECD is without prejudice to the status of the Golan Heights, East Jerusalem and Israeli settlements in the West Bank under the terms of international law.

Russian Federation: Regarding data from the Russian Federation in the Survey of Adult Skills (PIAAC), readers should note that the sample does not include the population of the Moscow municipal area. The data published, therefore, do not represent the entire resident population aged 16-65 in Russia but rather the population of Russia excluding the population residing in the Moscow municipal area. More detailed information regarding the data from the Russian Federation as well as that of other countries can be found in the *Technical Report of the Survey of Adult Skills* (OECD, forthcoming).

Notes to tables and charts

For further details on the data behind any figure, see the relevant indicator in the full publication *Education at a Glance 2014*, or click the hyperlink in the figure's source to download the data and notes.

1. EDUCATION LEVELS AND STUDENT NUMBERS

To what level have adults studied?

Who participates in education?

What is the role of early childhood education?

How many young people finish secondary education?

Does parental education affect students' chances?

To what level have adults studied?

- *About 75% of adults on average in OECD countries have attained at least upper secondary education.*
- *In some OECD countries, younger adults have higher tertiary attainment rates than older adults, leading by more than 20 percentage points on average.*
- *Women aged 25-34 have higher attainment rates in both upper secondary and tertiary education than men of the same age.*

Significance

Education is important both for the present and for the future. The level to which adults have studied is often used as a measure of human capital and the level of an individual's skills – in other words the skills available in the population and labour force. Higher levels of educational attainment are strongly associated with better health, more social engagement and higher employment rates, and are seen as a gateway to better jobs and higher relative earnings. Individuals have strong incentives to pursue more education, and governments have incentives to build on the skills of the population through education.

Findings

Almost all OECD countries have seen significant increases in educational attainment in recent decades, with upper secondary attainment becoming the norm and tertiary education on the rise. About 80% of younger adults have attained at least upper secondary education compared with 75% of all adults. On average, about 45% of the adult population across OECD countries have attained an upper secondary education as their highest qualification; this figure reaches more than 60% in Austria, the Czech Republic, Hungary, Latvia, Poland and the Slovak Republic. Gender differences in educational attainment have also evolved over the years. On average, 84% of younger women today have attained at least an upper secondary education compared with 81% of younger men.

Even if tertiary attainment rates have increased by 10 percentage points, among OECD countries since 2000, only about 34% of adult women and 31% of adult men attain tertiary education. In some OECD countries, younger adults have higher rates of tertiary education than older adults, especially among younger women who lead older women by an average of more than 20 percentage points in all countries. In some countries, the difference between generations is significant. In Korea, for example, there is a 52 percentage-point gap between these two age groups in tertiary attainment levels. By contrast, in Germany, Israel and the United States, difference between age groups is less than 3 percentage points.

In 2000, more men had university-level education than women. In 2012, the situation was reversed: 34% of women had attained a tertiary education compared with 31% of men. Tertiary attainment rates among young women are highest in Australia, Belgium, Canada, Denmark, Estonia, Ireland, Israel, Japan, Korea, Latvia, Luxembourg, New Zealand, Norway, Poland, the Russian Federation, Sweden and the United Kingdom, where at least one in two young women have attained tertiary education.

Trends

Efforts to raise people's level of education have led to significant changes in attainment rates, particularly at the top and bottom ends of the education spectrum. Between 2000 and 2012, the proportion of people without upper secondary or post-secondary non-tertiary education shrank at an average annual rate of about 3% while tertiary attainment increased by more than 3% each year. For the first time, in 2012, about one in three adults in OECD countries held a tertiary qualification. Upper secondary and post-secondary non-tertiary attainment levels have remained stable.

Definitions

"Adults" refers to the 25-64 year-old population; "younger adults" refers to 25-34 year-olds; "older adults" refers to 55-64 year-olds.

Data on population and education attainment for most countries are taken from OECD and Eurostat databases, which are compiled from National Labour Force Surveys.

Information on data for Israel:
http://dx.doi.org/10.1787/888932315602.

Going further

For additional material, notes and a full explanation of sourcing and methodologies, see *Education at a Glance 2014* (Indicator A1).

Areas covered include:

- Educational attainment of adults, by age and by gender.
- Adult skills and educational attainment (see Special chapter: Skills for life, p. 71).

Further reading from OECD

Reviews of National Policies for Education (series).

Figure 1.1. **Population that has attained tertiary education, 2012**

This figure shows the percentage of 25-64 year-olds who have been through tertiary education.

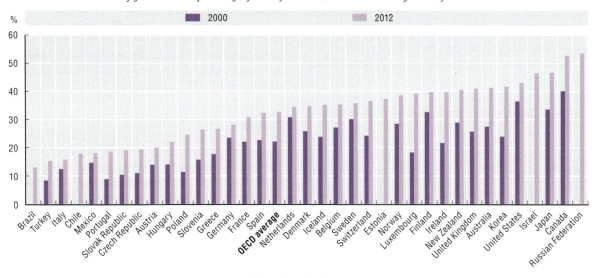

Source: OECD (2014), *Education at a Glance 2014*, Chart A1.1, available at *http://dx.doi.org/10.1787/888933114951*.

Figure 1.2. **Percentage-point difference between younger and older tertiary-educated adults, 2012**

This figure shows the percentage-point difference between the proportion of 25-34 year-olds and 55-64 year-olds who have attained tertiary education. The rapid expansion of education in recent decades means younger people tend to have higher levels of education.

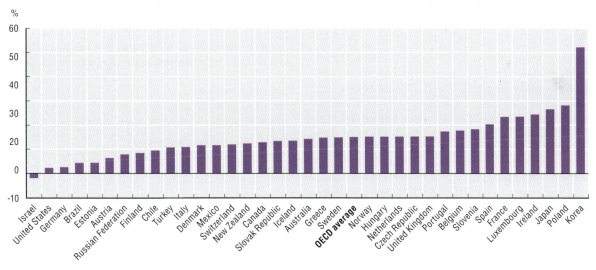

Source: OECD (2014), *Education at a Glance 2014*, Chart A1.3, available at *http://dx.doi.org/10.1787/888933114989*.

Who participates in education?

- *Access to education for 5-14 year-olds is universal in all OECD and most partner countries with available data.*
- *Enrolment rates among 15-19 year-olds are above 75% in 34 of the 40 OECD and partner countries with available data.*
- *Enrolment rates among 20-29 year-olds increased by 10 percentage points on average between 1995 and 2012 among OECD countries.*
- *More than 20% of 20-29 year-olds in all OECD countries, except Luxembourg, Mexico and the United Kingdom, were in education in 2012.*

Significance

The deep structural changes that have occurred in the global labour market over the past decades suggest that better-educated individuals will continue to have an advantage as the labour market becomes increasingly more knowledge-based. Education systems need to instil the skills students need to make them employable and enable them to pursue lifelong learning throughout their working lives. This section examines the evolution in access to education from 1995 to 2012, focussing on the number of young people who continue studying once compulsory education has ended.

Findings

Most people of school age in OECD countries have participated in an average 13 years of formal education, and this is increasing – a 5-year-old in an OECD country in 2012 could expect to participate in more than 17 years of education, on average, before reaching the age of 40. The expected duration of education ranged from more than 13 years in India and Indonesia to more than 19 years in Australia, Denmark, Finland, Iceland and Sweden. Women can expect to be enrolled in full-time education for 17 years while men can expect to be enrolled for 16 years, on average.

Compulsory education corresponds to primary and lower secondary programmes in all OECD countries, and upper secondary education in most of these countries. Between the ages of 5 and 14, enrolment rates are higher than 90%, i.e. there is universal coverage of basic education in all OECD and most partner countries with available data.

Based on 2012 data, enrolment rates among 15-19 year-olds were at least 80% in 29 of the 42 OECD and partner countries with available data, and 90% or higher in Belgium, the Czech Republic, Germany, Hungary, Ireland, Latvia, the Netherlands, Poland and Slovenia.

In 2012, an average of 28% of 20-29 year-olds in OECD countries were enrolled in some type of education. The highest proportions of this age group enrolled in education (more than 40%) are found in Denmark, Finland, Greece and Iceland. The only countries with less than 15% are Colombia, Indonesia, Luxembourg, Mexico and South Africa. Among 20-29 year-olds, 30% of women and 27% of men participate in education in OECD countries.

Trends

Between 1995 and 2012, enrolment rates for 15-19 year-olds in OECD countries increased steadily by around 10 percentage points, from an average 74% to 84%. While rates increased by close to 30 percentage points during this period in Turkey, and by more than 20 percentage points in the Czech Republic, Greece and Hungary, they remained virtually unchanged in Belgium (about 94%) and Germany (about 90%). In France, the enrolment rate for this age group fell from 89% to 84% during this period. There has been growth, too, in enrolment rates for 20-29 year-olds. From 1995 to 2012, the enrolment rate for this segment of the population has grown by 10 percentage points on average among OECD countries.

Definitions

Data for the 2011-12 school year are based on the UOE data collection on education statistics, administered annually by the OECD. Except where otherwise noted, figures are based on head counts and do not distinguish between full-time and part-time study because the concept of part-time study is not recognised by some countries.

Information on data for Israel:
http://dx.doi.org/10.1787/888932315602.

> ### Going further
>
> For additional material, notes and a full explanation of sourcing and methodologies, see *Education at a Glance 2014* (Indicator C1).
>
> Areas covered include:
>
> – Students in primary, secondary and tertiary education, by type of institution or mode of enrolment.
> – Proportion of young adults in education.
> – Expected number of years in education.

Figure 1.3. **Enrolment rates of 15-19 year-olds (1995, 2012)**

This figure shows the increase or decrease in the percentage of 15-19 year-olds enrolled in full-time and part-time education.

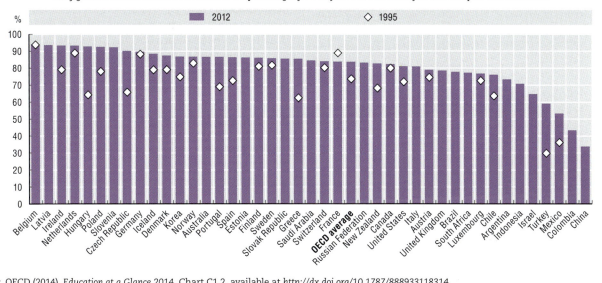

Source: OECD (2014), *Education at a Glance 2014*, Chart C1.2, available at *http://dx.doi.org/10.1787/888933118314*.

Figure 1.4. **Enrolment rates of 20-29 year-olds (1995, 2012)**

This figure shows the increase in the percentage of 20-29 year-olds enrolled in full-time and part-time education.

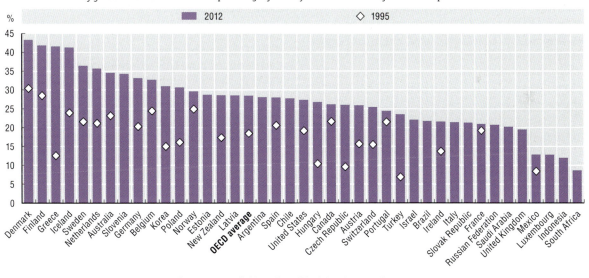

Source: OECD (2014), *Education at a Glance 2014*, Chart C1.1, available at *http://dx.doi.org/10.1787/888933118295*.

What is the role of early childhood education?

- *Fifteen-year-olds who had at least one year of pre-primary education perform better at school.*

- *Early childhood education has grown alongside the increase in women working in many OECD countries, but improving access without improving the quality of these services will not ensure good results.*

- *Education now begins for most children in OECD countries well before they are 5 years old. In Belgium, Denmark, France, Germany, Iceland, Italy, Norway, Spain, Sweden and the United Kingdom, more than 90% of 3-year-olds are enrolled in early childhood education.*

- *More than three-quarters of 4-year-olds (84%) are enrolled in early childhood education and primary education in OECD countries; the figure is 89% for OECD countries that are part of the European Union.*

Significance

Early childhood education plays a key role in cognitive and emotional development. Enrolling pupils in early childhood education can also mitigate social inequalities and promote better student outcomes overall. As a result, ensuring the quality of early childhood education and care has become a policy priority in many countries.

As countries continue to expand their early childhood programmes, they need to consider parents' needs and expectations regarding accessibility, cost, programme and staff quality, and accountability.

Findings

Results from the OECD's Programme for International Student Assessment (PISA) show that, in most countries, pupils who have attended pre-primary education programmes tend to perform better at age 15 than those who have not.

An increase in women working outside the home, and having children later in life, have gone hand in hand with an increase in early childhood education. The average age at which mothers have their first child has risen across all OECD countries, except Mexico, over the past 40 years.

Spending on pre-primary education accounts for an average of 0.6% of gross domestic product (GDP), although there are significant differences between countries. While 0.1% of GDP is spent on pre-primary education in Australia, about 0.8% or more is spent in Chile, Denmark, Iceland, Latvia, Luxembourg, the Russian Federation, Slovenia and Spain.

Publicly funded pre-primary education tends to be more strongly developed in European countries than elsewhere in the OECD. Private expenditure varies widely between countries, ranging from 5% or less in Belgium, Estonia, Latvia, Luxembourg and Sweden, to 25% or more in Argentina, Australia, Austria, Colombia, Japan, Korea, Spain and the United States.

Public spending on pre-primary education is mainly used to support public institutions, but it also funds private institutions. On average among OECD countries, the level of public expenditure on public pre-primary institutions, at USD 6 460 per pupil, is around twice the level of public spending on private pre-primary institutions (USD 3 618).

The ratio of pupils to teaching staff is also an important indicator of the resources devoted to pre-primary education. The pupil-teacher ratio excluding non-teaching staff (e.g. teachers' aides) ranges from more than 20 pupils per teacher in Chile, France, Indonesia, Israel, Mexico and Turkey, to fewer than 10 in Estonia, Iceland, New Zealand, Slovenia and Sweden.

Trends

Enrolment in early childhood education programmes rose from 64% of 3-year-olds in 2005 to 71% in 2012 on average for OECD countries, and from 79% of 4-year-olds in 2005 to 84% in 2012. In Australia, Brazil and Poland, enrolment rates of 4-year-olds increased by 20 percentage points or more during this period.

Definitions

Early childhood education, or pre-primary education (ISCED 0), is defined as the initial stage of *organised instruction*, designed primarily to introduce very young children to a school-like environment.

Information on data for Israel:
http://dx.doi.org/10.1787/888932315602.

Going further

For additional material, notes and a full explanation of sourcing and methodologies, see *Education at a Glance 2014* (Indicator C2).

Areas covered include:

- Enrolment rates in pre-primary programmes.
- Public and private spending on pre-primary education.
- Influence of pre-primary education policies on Programme for International Student Assessment (PISA) results.

Further reading from OECD

OECD (2011), *Starting Strong III: A Quality Toolbox for Early Childhood Education and Care,* OECD Publishing, Paris, *http://dx.doi.org/10.1787/9789264123564-en.*

Figure 1.5. **Enrolment rates in education at age 3 (2005, 2012)**

This figure compares the 2005 and 2012 enrolment rates (full-time and part-time) of 3-year-olds in public and private institutions.

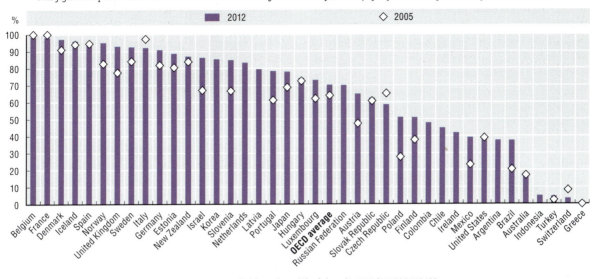

Source: OECD (2014), *Education at a Glance 2014*, Chart C2.1 available at *http://dx.doi.org/0.1787/888933118409.*

Figure 1.6. **Ratio of students to teaching staff in early childhood education, 2012**

This figure shows the number of students per teacher in early childhood education.

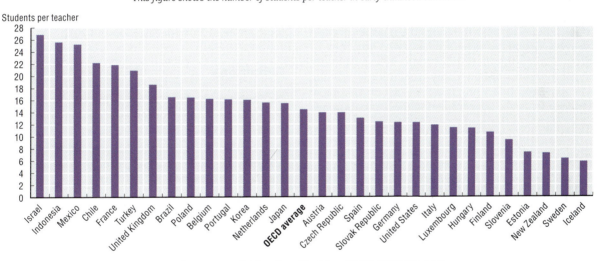

Source: OECD (2014), *Education at a Glance 2014*, Chart C2.4 available at *http://dx.doi.org/10.1787/888933118466.*

How many young people finish secondary education?

- *On average 84% of today's young people in OECD countries are expected to complete upper secondary education over their lifetimes, based on current patterns of graduation. For G20 countries, the level is 80%.*

- *Young women are now more likely than young men to graduate from upper secondary programmes in almost all OECD countries, a reversal of the historical pattern.*

- *More than 10% of upper secondary graduates in Denmark, Finland, the Netherlands and Norway are 25 or older while in Iceland nearly 20% of them are.*

Significance

This section shows how many students are expected to finish secondary education. Upper secondary education, aims to equip students with the basic skills and knowledge necessary to enter the labour market or tertiary education, and to become engaged citizens. Graduating from upper secondary education has become increasingly important in all countries, as the skills needed in the labour market are becoming more knowledge-based and as workers are progressively required to adapt to the uncertainties of a rapidly changing global economy. Young people in OECD countries who do not finish secondary education face severe difficulties when it comes to finding work. Policy makers are examining ways to reduce the number of early school-leavers, defined as those students who do not complete their upper secondary education. Internationally comparable measures of how many students successfully complete upper secondary programmes – which also show how many students are not completing these programmes – can assist efforts to that end.

Findings

First-time upper secondary graduation rates equal or exceed 75% in 25 of 31 countries with available data. In Denmark, Finland, Germany, Hungary, Iceland, Ireland, Japan, Korea, Latvia, the Netherlands, Slovenia, Spain and the United Kingdom, graduation rates equal or exceed 90%. Graduation rates for women now average 87% compared with 81% for men.

Among countries with available data, 72% of students who begin upper secondary education complete the programmes they entered within the theoretical duration of the programme. However, there are large differences in completion rates, depending on gender and type of programme. This also varies by country, as 95% of students in Korea complete their education in the stipulated time, whereas only 40% do in Luxembourg.

Students graduate for the first time at upper secondary level at the age of 20, on average among OECD countries. However, this age varies between countries: from 17 years in Israel, New Zealand, Turkey and the United States to 22 or older in Iceland and Norway.

Traditionally, more men have graduated from pre-vocational and vocational programmes than women, but more young women are graduating from vocational programmes and approaching the graduation rates of their male counterparts. Today the average graduation rate for vocational programmes is 50% for men compared with 46% for women. And in Belgium, Denmark, Finland, Ireland, the Netherlands and Spain, graduation rates for women are at least 5 percentage points higher than those for men.

Gender differences are also apparent in young people's choice of field of study when pursuing vocational education. Engineering, manufacturing and construction are by far the most popular fields of study for boys, (almost half of them chose these fields in 2012). On the other hand, girls are more dispersed among social sciences, business and law (24%), health and welfare (19%), and services (19%).

Trends

Since 2000, upper secondary graduation rates have increased by an average of almost 8 percentage points among OECD countries with comparable data. The greatest increase occurred in Mexico, which showed an annual growth rate of 3% between 2000 and 2012.

Definitions

Data refer to the 2011-12 academic year and are based on the UOE data collection on education statistics administered by the OECD in 2012.

Data on trends in graduation rates at upper secondary level for the years 1995 and 2000 through 2004 are based on a special survey carried out in January 2007.

Information on data for Israel:
http://dx.doi.org/10.1787/888932315602.

Going further

For additional material, notes and a full explanation of sourcing and methodologies, see *Education at a Glance 2014 (Indicator A2).*

Areas covered include:

- Current upper secondary graduation rates and trends.
- Successful completion of upper secondary programmes, by programme orientation and gender.

Figure 1.7. **Upper secondary graduation rates, 2012**

*This figure shows the percentage of students who enter an upper secondary programme for the first time
and who graduate from it in the amount of time normally allocated for completing the programme.*

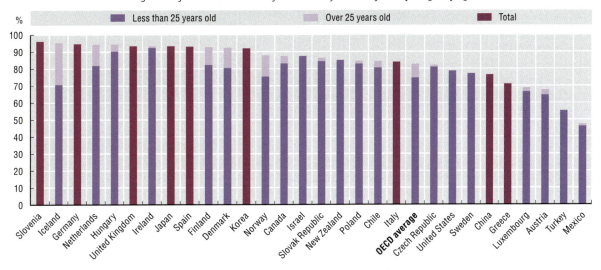

Source: OECD (2014), *Education at a Glance 2014*, Chart A2.1, available at *http://dx.doi.org/10.1787/888933115255*.

Figure 1.8. **Average age of upper secondary graduates, 2012**

This figure shows the average age of students who enter and successfully complete an upper secondary programme.

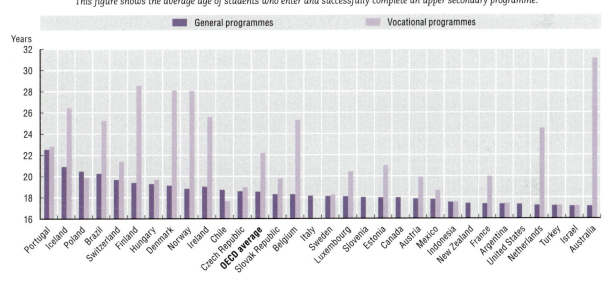

Source: OECD (2014), *Education at a Glance 2014*, Chart A2.2, available at *http://dx.doi.org/10.1787/888933115274*.

Does parental education affect students' chances?

- *About 40% of non-student adults have a higher level of educational attainment than their parents, on average.*
- *Women are more successful than men in attaining a higher level of education than their parents. Some 40% of women and 38% of men have a higher level of educational attainment than their parents, on average.*
- *More than 30% of non-student adults whose parents have not attained upper secondary education did not attain this level of education themselves.*

Significance

Because of its strong links to earnings, employment, overall wealth and the well-being of individuals, education can reduce inequalities in societies, but it can also reproduce them. Giving all young people a fair chance to obtain a quality education is a fundamental part of the social contract. Addressing inequalities in education opportunities is critically important for maintaining social mobility and broadening the pool of candidates for higher education and high-skilled jobs.

Findings

Tertiary education attainment rates have been growing in recent years, especially among younger generations. On average among countries, about 40% of adults have a higher level of educational attainment than their parents. Intergenerational educational upward mobility is the highest in Finland, Flanders (Belgium), Korea and the Russian Federation, where more than 55% of adults have attained a higher level of education than their parents. On the contrary, 12% of non-student adults have lower educational attainment than their parents. In Austria, Denmark, Estonia, Germany, Norway, Sweden and the United States more than 15% of this population does.

More than 30% of non-student adults whose parents have not attained upper secondary education have not obtained it themselves. On average, at least 35% of 20-34 year-olds in tertiary education have at least one parent who has completed that level of education. In Canada, Estonia, Germany, Japan, Norway and Sweden, at least 65% of these students do. The likelihood of a student participating in tertiary education is twice as great if at least one of the parents attained upper secondary or post-secondary non-tertiary education, and about 4.5 times as great if both parents attained tertiary education. On average, only 9% of tertiary students have parents with low levels of education.

Women are slightly more likely than men to attain a higher level of education than their parents. But in Austria, Germany, Korea, and the Netherlands, men are considerably more upwardly mobile in educational attainment than women.

Trends

The expansion of education systems in many OECD countries, both at the upper secondary or post-secondary non-tertiary and tertiary levels of education, has given young people (25-34 year-olds) an opportunity to attain a higher level of education than their parents. On average, 32% of young people have achieved a higher level of education than their parents, while only 16% have not been able to reach their parents' education level, among OECD countries with available data. In all countries except Estonia, Germany, Norway and Sweden, upward mobility in education is more common than downward mobility, reflecting the expansion of education systems in most OECD countries. The expansion of education has been particularly pronounced in France, Ireland, Italy, Korea, Spain and the Russian Federation, where the difference between upward and downward educational mobility for the 25-34 year-olds is 30 percentage points or more.

Definitions

"Adults" refers to 25-64 year-olds.

All data are based on the Survey of Adult Skills (PIAAC) 2012. PIAAC is the OECD Programme for the International Assessment of Adult Competencies.

Information on data for Israel:
http://dx.doi.org/10.1787/888932315602.

Going further

For additional material, notes and a full explanation of sourcing and methodologies, see *Education at a Glance 2014* (Indicator A4).

Areas covered include:

- Odds of attending higher education if parents are highly educated.
- Intergenerational mobility.

Further reading from OECD

OECD (2013), *PISA 2012 Results: Excellence through Equity (Volume II): Giving Every Student the Chance to Succeed*, PISA, OECD Publishing, Paris, *http://dx.doi.org/10.1787/9789264201132-en.*

OECD (2012), *Let's Read Them a Story! The Parent Factor in Education*, PISA, OECD Publishing, Paris, *http://dx.doi.org/10.1787/9789264176232-en.*

Figure 1.9. **Percentage of 20-34 year-olds in tertiary education, by parents' education level, 2012**

Countries are ranked in descending order of the participation in tertiary education of 20-34 year-olds that have parents with tertiary attainment.

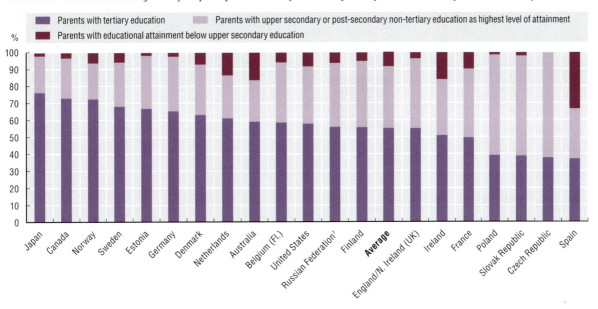

1. Data do not include Moscow municipal area.
Source: OECD (2014), *Education at a Glance 2014*, Chart A4.1, available at *http://dx.doi.org/10.1787/888933115635.*

Figure 1.10. **Intergenerational mobility in education, 2012**

This figure shows the percentage of 25-64 year-old non-students whose educational attainment is higher than (upward mobility), lower than (downward mobility) or the same as (status quo) that of their parents.

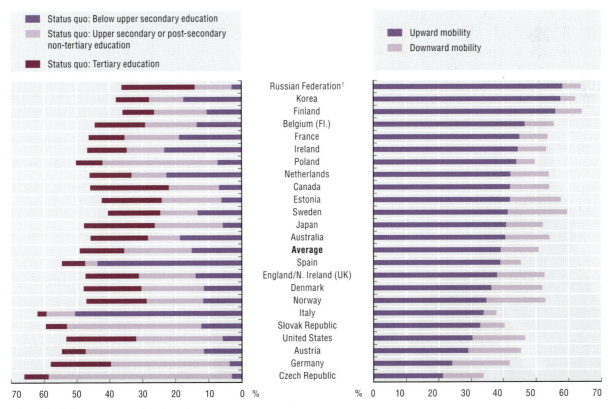

1. Data do not include Moscow municipal area.
Source: OECD (2014), *Education at a Glance 2014*, Chart A4.3, available at *http://dx.doi.org/10.1787/888933115673.*

2. HIGHER EDUCATION AND WORK

How many young people enter tertiary education?

How many young people graduate from tertiary education?

How many students study abroad and where do they go?

How successful are students in moving from education to work?

How many young people enter tertiary education?

- *Some 58% of young adults in OECD countries are expected to enter university-level programmes over their lifetimes; however less than 3% are expected to enter advanced research programmes.*
- *Social sciences, business and law are the most popular fields of university-level study in almost all countries.*
- *Entry rates into university-level programmes are still higher for women (65%) than for men (52%) on average among OECD countries. But in advanced research programmes the gender gap almost disappears.*

Significance

This section shows how many students are expected to enter a specific type of tertiary education during their lifetimes. It also sheds light on the accessibility and perceived value of tertiary programmes, and provides some indication of the degree to which a population is acquiring the high-level skills and knowledge valued by today's labour market. High entry and enrolment rates in tertiary education imply that a highly educated labour force is being developed and maintained.

Findings

An estimated 58% of young adults in OECD countries will enter university level programmes during their lifetimes if current patterns of entry continue. In several countries, at least 70% of young adults are expected to enter these programmes, while less than 35% are expected to do so in Belgium, Luxembourg and Mexico. This is also true of China and Indonesia among other G20 countries.

However, the number of entrants is somewhat different if international students who come to a country to study are excluded. In Australia, there is a 26 percentage point drop. However, in Poland and Slovenia the entry rate remains at around 70%.

Less than 3% of today's young adults in OECD countries are expected to enter advanced research programmes during their lifetimes. The proportions range from 1% or less in Chile, Japan, Luxembourg and Mexico (as well as Argentina and Indonesia among other G20 countries), to around 5% in Germany and Switzerland.

It is estimated that 18% of today's young adults (20% of women and 17% of men) will enter vocational programmes over their lifetimes. Proportions range from less than 5% in Iceland, Indonesia, Mexico, Poland and the Slovak Republic, to more than 35% in Belgium, Korea and New Zealand, and above 50% in Argentina and Chile.

On average among OECD countries, 82% of first-time entrants into university-level programmes and 58% of first-time entrants into vocationally-oriented programmes in 2012 were under 25 years of age. In addition, 57% of students who entered advanced research programmes in 2012 were under 30 years of age.

The most popular fields of study chosen by new entrants into tertiary programmes are social sciences, business and law in all countries except Finland, Korea and Saudi Arabia.

Trends

The proportion of students entering university-level education increased by more than 20 percentage points, on average in OECD countries between 1995 and 2012. There has been a marked decrease of 4 percentage points since 2010, probably caused by the financial crisis. The overall increase since 1995 was due to the increased accessibility of tertiary education in many countries, but also because of structural changes in the education systems of some countries. Entry rates for tertiary programmes have also increased because the source of applicants has expanded to include many more international and older students.

Definitions

Data refer to the academic year 2011-12 and are based on the UOE data collection on education statistics administered by the OECD in 2013. Data on trends in entry rates for the years 1995, 2000, 2001, 2002, 2003 and 2004 are based on a special survey carried out in OECD countries in January 2007. Data on the impact of international students on tertiary entry rates are based on a special survey carried out by the OECD in December 2013. The net entry rate for a specific age is obtained by dividing the number of entrants of that age to each type of tertiary education by the total population in the corresponding age group.

Information on data for Israel:
http://dx.doi.org/10.1787/888932315602.

Going further

For additional material, notes and a full explanation of sourcing and methodologies, see *Education at a Glance 2014* (Indicator C3).

Areas covered include:

- Entry rates by level of education.
- Age of new entrants in tertiary education.
- Distribution of new entrants by age and gender.

Figure 2.1. **Entry rates into university-level education (2000, 2012)**

This figure shows the growth – or otherwise – in the percentage of young people entering university-level education. Entry rates have risen in most OECD countries.

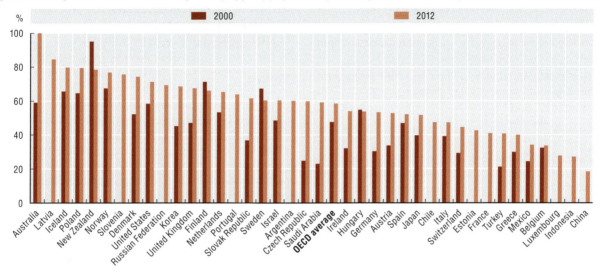

Source: OECD (2014), *Education at a Glance 2014*, Chart C3.2., available at *http://dx.doi.org/10.1787/888933118599*.

Figure 2.2. **Entry rates into vocationally-oriented tertiary education (2000, 2012)**

This figure shows the percentage of young people entering vocationally-oriented tertiary education

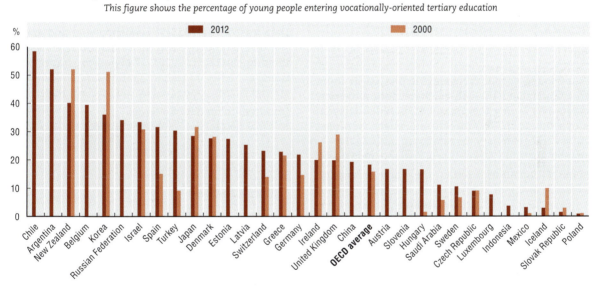

Source: OECD (2014), *Education at a Glance 2014*, Chart C3.2, available at *http://dx.doi.org/10.1787/888933118599*.

How many young people graduate from tertiary education?

- Some 39% of today's young adults in OECD countries are expected to complete university level education over their lifetimes, based on current patterns of graduation.

- About 11% of today's young adults in OECD countries are expected to complete vocationally-oriented education over their lifetimes.

- A student in an OECD country obtains his or her first university-level degree at the age of 27 on average.

Significance

Tertiary education rates indicate a country's capacity to equip future workers with specialised knowledge and skills. People have strong incentives to obtain a tertiary education in OECD countries, including higher salaries and better employment prospects. Tertiary education varies widely in structure and scope between countries, and graduation rates are influenced by the ease of access to these programmes, flexibility in completing them and the demand for higher skills in the labour market. Expanding access to and improving the quality of tertiary education are vital to knowledge-based economies, but these objectives are even more difficult to achieve when budgets are tight.

Findings

Some 39% of young people, on average across OECD countries with comparable data, will graduate from university level programmes during their lifetimes, based on current patterns of graduation. The proportion ranges from less than 25% in Chile, Hungary, Luxembourg and Mexico, to 50% or more in Australia, Iceland, New Zealand and Poland.

Students in OECD countries obtain their first university-level degree at the age of 27 on average, with ages ranging from less than 25 in Belgium, Luxembourg, Mexico, the Netherlands and the United Kingdom to more than 29 in Brazil, Finland, Iceland, Israel and Sweden.

Most graduates of tertiary education programmes are women, except at the doctoral level. An estimated 47% of women and 31% of men on average in OECD countries will complete university level education over their lifetimes, based on current patterns of graduation.

Some 1.6% of young people today are expected to complete advanced research programmes on average among OECD countries, up from 1.0% in 2000. Countries with the highest increase in graduation rates from advanced research programmes are the Czech Republic, Denmark, Ireland, Italy, New Zealand, Norway, the Slovak Republic and the United Kingdom, where graduation rates increased by at least 1 percentage point from 2000 to 2012.

International students represent a significant share of tertiary graduates in a number of countries. For example, when international students are excluded, first-degree tertiary graduation rates drop by 18 percentage points for Australia and 11 points for New Zealand.

Trends

University-level graduation rates have risen by 22 percentage points on average across OECD countries with available data over the past 17 years, while rates for vocationally oriented tertiary programmes have remained stable. Doctorates represent only a small proportion of tertiary programmes but the graduation rate has doubled over the same period, from 0.8% to 1.6%.

Definitions

Tertiary graduates are those who obtain a university degree, vocational qualifications, or advanced research degrees of doctorate standard. Net graduation rates represent the estimated percentage of an age group that will complete tertiary education over their lifetimes, based on current patterns of graduation.

Data are for the 2011-12 academic year and are based on the UOE data collection on education statistics administered by the OECD in 2012. Data on the impact of international students on tertiary graduation rates are based on a special survey conducted by the OECD in December 2013.

Information on data for Israel:
http://dx.doi.org/10.1787/888932315602.

Going further

For additional material, notes and a full explanation of sourcing and methodologies, see *Education at a Glance 2014* (Indicator A3).

Areas covered include:

– Graduation rates by level of qualification, age, gender and field of study.

Further reading from OECD

Higher Education Management and Policy (journal).

OECD Reviews of Tertiary Education (series of national reviews).

OECD Reviews of Higher Education in Regional and City Development (series).

Figure 2.3. **First-time graduation rates from university-level education (1995, 2012)**

This figure shows the growth in the percentage of first-time graduates from university-level education.

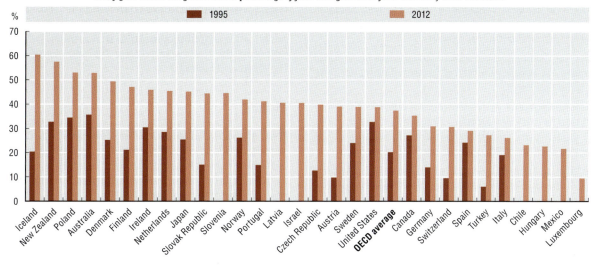

Source: OECD (2014), *Education at a Glance 2014*, Chart A3.2, available at *http://dx.doi.org/10.1787/888933115483*.

Figure 2.4. **First-time graduation rates from vocationally oriented education (1995, 2012)**

This figure shows the growth or decline in the percentage of first-time graduates from vocationally oriented tertiary education.

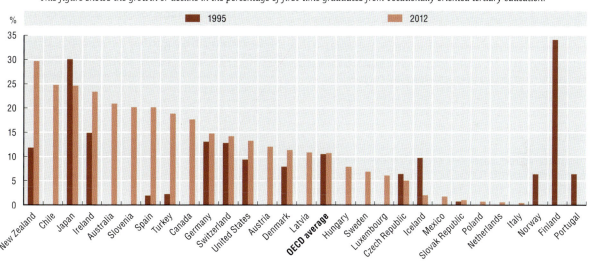

Source: OECD (2014), *Education at a Glance 2014*, Chart A3.2, available at *http://dx.doi.org/10.1787/888933115483*.

How many students study abroad and where do they go?

- *More than 4.5 million students are enrolled in university-level education outside their home country. Australia, Austria, Luxembourg, New Zealand, Switzerland and the United Kingdom have the highest proportion of international students as a percentage of their total tertiary enrolments.*

- *Students from Asia represent 53% of foreign students enrolled worldwide. The largest numbers of foreign students are from China, India and Korea.*

- *OECD countries receive more international students than they send abroad for tertiary education. About three times as many foreign students are enrolled in tertiary education in OECD countries as there are OECD citizens studying abroad.*

- *Some 82% of all foreign students are enrolled in G20 countries, while 75% are enrolled in OECD countries. These proportions have remained stable during the past decade.*

Significance

This section looks at the extent to which students are studying abroad and their preferred destinations. Pursuing higher-level education in a foreign country allows students to expand their knowledge of other societies and languages, and thus improve their prospects in globalised sectors of the labour market. Beyond its social and educational effects, studying abroad has a considerable economic impact. For host countries, enrolling international students can not only help raise revenues from higher education, but also can be part of a broader strategy to recruit highly skilled immigrants.

Findings

OECD countries attract three out of four students studying abroad, with Australia, Canada, France, Germany, the United Kingdom and the United States together receiving more than 50% of all foreign students worldwide.

In terms of geographical area, Europe is the top destination for tertiary level students enrolled outside their country of origin, hosting 48% of these students, followed by North America, which hosts 21% of all international students and Asia with 18%. The number of international students in Oceania has tripled since 2000, although this region hosts less than 10% of all foreign students. Other regions, such as Africa, Latin America and the Caribbean, are also seeing growing numbers of international students, reflecting the internationalisation of universities in an increasing number of countries.

International students from OECD countries mainly come from Canada, France, Germany, Italy, Korea and the United States. In the 21 European countries that are members of the OECD, there were, on average, three foreign students per European citizen enrolled abroad.

International students represent 10% or more of the enrolments in tertiary education in Australia, Austria, Luxembourg, New Zealand, Switzerland and the United Kingdom. They also account for more than 30% of enrolments in advanced research programmes in Australia, Belgium, Luxembourg, the Netherlands, New Zealand, Switzerland, and the United Kingdom.

Trends

Over the past three decades, the number of students enrolled outside their country of citizenship has risen dramatically, from 0.8 million worldwide in 1975 to 4.5 million in 2012, a more than fivefold increase. During 2000-2012, the number of foreign tertiary students enrolled worldwide more than doubled, with an average annual growth rate of almost 7%. In OECD countries, the number of foreign students enrolled at the tertiary level mirrored the global trend.

Definitions

Students are classified as "international" if they left their country of origin and moved to another country to study. Students are classified as "foreign" if they are not citizens of the country in which they are studying. Data on international and foreign students refer to the academic year 2011-12 unless otherwise indicated and are based on the UOE data collection on education statistics administered by the OECD in 2012. Additional data from the UNESCO Institute for Statistics are also included.

Information on data for Israel: *http://dx.doi.org/10.1787/888932315602.*

Going further

For additional material, notes and a full explanation of sourcing and methodologies, see *Education at a Glance 2014* (Indicator C4).

Areas covered include:

- Distribution of students by country of origin and destination.
- Trends in the numbers of students studying abroad.

Further reading from OECD

OECD (2013), *International Migration Outlook 2013*, OECD Publishing, Paris, *http://dx.doi.org/10.1787/migr_outlook-2013-en.*

Figure 2.5. **Trends in international education market shares (2000, 2012)**

This figure shows the distribution of foreign and international students in tertiary education, by destination.

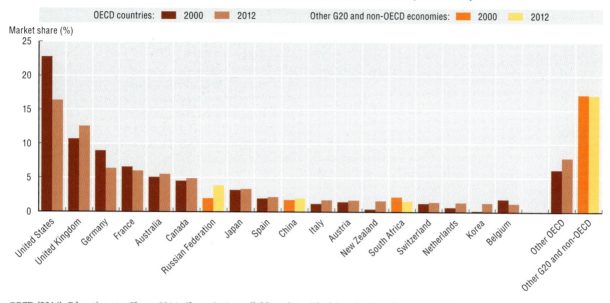

Source: OECD (2014), *Education at a Glance 2014*, Chart C4.3, available at *http://dx.doi.org/10.1787/888933118827*.

Figure 2.6. **Student mobility in tertiary education, 2012**

This figure shows the percentage of international students at the tertiary level in each country.

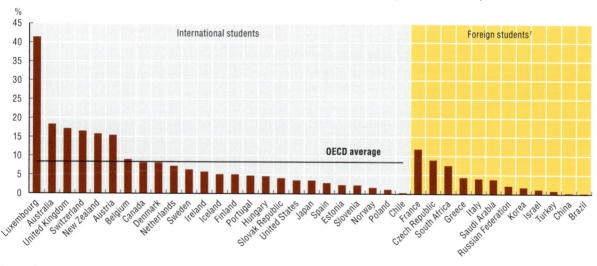

1. Foreign students are defined on the basis if their country of citizenship, these data are not comparable with data on the international students and are therefore presented separately in the chart.

Source: OECD (2014), *Education at a Glance 2014*, Chart C4.4 available at *http://dx.doi.org/10.1787/888933118846*.

How successful are students in moving from education to work?

- *About 15% of people aged 15-29 are not employed nor in education and training (NEET) on average in OECD countries; women are more likely to be NEET than men.*
- *The proportion of 15-29 year-olds not in education who had a job shrank from 41% in 2008 to 36% in 2012, on average among OECD countries.*
- *On average among OECD countries, about 50% of 15-29 year-olds working part time would like to work more.*

Significance

This section illustrates the difficulty of moving from education to work for the younger generation today. During recessionary periods, fewer job vacancies make the transition from school to work substantially more difficult for young people, as those with more work experience are favoured over new entrants into the labour market. This section looks at the number of years young people can be expected to spend in education, employment and non-employment. To improve the transition of young people from school to work, regardless of the economic climate, education systems should work to ensure that people have the skills that are needed in the labour market.

Findings

Almost half (49%) of 15-29 year-olds were in education on average among OECD countries in 2012. Of the remaining 51%, 36% held a job, 7% were unemployed and 8% were outside the labour force. In Chile, Ireland, Italy, Mexico, Spain and Turkey, more than 20% of 15-29 year-olds are neither employed nor in education and training.

A typical 15-year-old in an OECD country in 2012 could expect to spend about 7 additional years in formal education during the next 15 years. In addition, before turning 30, he or she could expect to hold a job for over five years, to be unemployed for nearly one year, and to be out of the labour force – that is, neither in education nor seeking work – for over one year.

About one in two 15-29 year-olds in OECD countries is employed. Some 8% of these young people work part time while studying; 5% work part time but are no longer studying; 6% work full time while studying; and 30% work full time and are no longer in education.

Women between 15 and 29 years old are twice as likely as men of the same age to be completely out of the labour force. They can expect to spend 1.7 years in this situation, compared to 0.8 years for men.

Trends:

Efforts by governments to raise people's level of education have led to significant changes in educational participa-tion. In 2000, an average of 41% of 15-29 year-olds in OECD countries were in education; by 2012, that proportion had risen to 49%. While the percentage of individuals in education increased steadily between 2000 and 2012, trends in youth employment have been marked by two periods of large drops: between 2000 and 2003 (-3.3 percentage points) and between 2008 and 2012 (-4.4 percentage points). These decreases in youth employment coincided with the slow-down in economic activity in the early 2000s and the reces-sion triggered by the global financial crisis in 2008. The proportion of 15-29 year-olds not employed nor in educa-tion or training (NEET) remained stable at around 15% between 2000 and 2012.

Definitions

Employed refers to individuals who have a job or are at work for one hour or more in paid employment or self-employment. Full-time worker refers to those working usu-ally 30 hours or more on their main job. Data for most countries are taken from OECD and Eurostat databases, which are compiled from National Labour Force Surveys by the OECD LSO (Labour Market and Social Outcomes of Learning) Network, and usually refer to the first quarter, or the average of the first three months of the calendar year. Some discrepancies may exist in the data collected.

Information on data for Israel:
http://dx.doi.org/10.1787/888932315602.

Going further

For additional material, notes and a full explanation of sourcing and methodologies, see *Education at a Glance 2014* (Indicator C5).

Areas covered include:

- Expected years in education and not in education for 15-29 year-olds, as well as trends and gender dif-ferences.
- Transition from school to work for different age groups.
- Voluntary/involuntary part-time work.

Further reading from OECD

OECD (2012), *Better Skills, Better Jobs, Better Lives: A Strategic Approach to Skills Policies*, OECD Publishing, Paris, *http://dx.doi.org/10.1787/9789264177338-en.*

Figure 2.7. **Young people not in education by labour market status, 2012**

This figure shows the work status of 15-19 year-olds not in education or training.

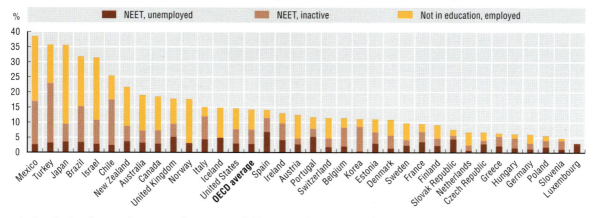

Source: OECD (2014), *Education at a Glance 2014*, Chart C5.3, available at *http://dx.doi.org/10.1787/888933119055*.

Figure 2.8. **Education and employment among young people, 2012**

These figures show the work status of 15-29 year-olds.

Source: OECD (2014), *Education at a Glance 2014*, Chart C5.2, available at *http://dx.doi.org/10.1787/888933119036*.

3. THE ECONOMIC AND SOCIAL BENEFITS OF EDUCATION

How does education affect employment rates?

How much more do tertiary graduates earn?

What are the incentives to invest in education?

How are student performance and equity in education related?

How does education affect employment rates?

- *People with a tertiary education in OECD countries are more likely to have a job, and to be working full-time, than those without.*
- *Unemployment rates are higher among people who do not have an upper secondary education (14% on average across OECD countries) than among those who have a tertiary education (5%).*
- *People with at least an upper secondary education are more likely to have a job than those without this level of education.*
- *The employment rate is considerably higher among men (80%) than among women (65%), although the gap is narrowest among tertiary-educated individuals and widest among those without an upper secondary education.*

Significance

This section examines the relationship between education and working life. OECD countries depend upon a sufficient supply of well-educated and skilled workers to promote economic development. Educational qualifications are frequently used to measure human capital and the level of an individual's skills. In most OECD countries people with high qualifications have the highest employment rates and people with the lowest educational qualifications are at greater risk of being unemployed.

Findings

Education has a substantial impact on employment prospects. On average among OECD countries, over 80% of the population with tertiary education is employed. The OECD average falls to over 70% for people with upper secondary or post-secondary non-tertiary education and to less than 60% for those without an upper secondary education. The probability of working full time also increases with the level of education. Some 64% of employed adults with below upper secondary education work full time, compared with 74% of the employed with a tertiary education.

Differences in employment rates between tertiary-educated individuals and those with below upper secondary education are particularly large in Austria, Belgium, the Czech Republic, Estonia, Germany, Hungary, Ireland, Israel, Poland, the Russian Federation, the Slovak Republic and Slovenia where they amount to at least 30 percentage points. Across all OECD countries and education levels, the employment rate of women is far below that of men at all levels of education: only 65% of women are employed compared with 80% of men. Although the gender gap narrows as educational attainment increases, the employment rate among tertiary-educated women is still considerably lower than that of men – despite the fact that in 2012 a slightly

higher proportion of women (34%) than men (31%) in OECD countries had received a tertiary education.

Individuals with a vocationally-oriented upper secondary or post-secondary education in OECD countries are more likely to be employed (75%) than those who have a general upper secondary degree (70%). They are also less likely to be unemployed (8%) than those with a general upper secondary degree (9%).

Trends

Over the past 15 years, employment rates for men and women with tertiary education have consistently been higher than for those without. Conversely, unemployment rates among lower-educated men and women have been higher than among those with tertiary education. Overall, younger adults struggle the most, and unemployment rates are highest among those who have only below upper secondary education. In 2012, about 20% of young adults in OECD countries were unemployed, the highest rate registered in more than a decade.

Definitions

The employment rate refers to the number of persons in employment as a percentage of the population of working age. The unemployment rate refers to unemployed persons as a percentage of the labour force. The unemployed are defined as people without work but actively seeking employment and currently available to start work. The employed are defined as those who work for pay or profit for at least one hour a week, or who have a job but are temporarily not at work due to illness, leave or industrial action.

Information on data for Israel:
http://dx.doi.org/10.1787/888932315602.

Going further

For additional material, notes and a full explanation of sourcing and methodologies, see *Education at a Glance 2014* (Indicator A5).

Areas covered include:

- Trends in employment and unemployment rates, by gender, age and educational attainment.
- Employment rates of individuals with vocational and general education.
- Part-time and involuntary part-time work.

Figure 3.1. **Employment rate of 25-64 year-olds, by education level, 2012**

This figure shows the employment rates of people according to their education levels.

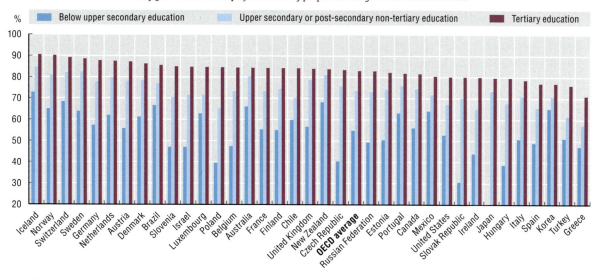

Source: OECD (2014), *Education at a Glance 2014*, Chart A5.1 at *http://dx.doi.org/10.1787/888933115958*.

Figure 3.2. **Unemployment rates among 25-64 year-olds with tertiary education (2005, 2010 and 2012)**

This figure shows the unemployment rates among 25-64 year-olds.

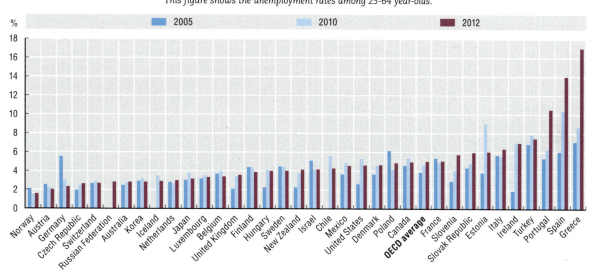

Source: OECD (2014), *Education at a Glance 2014*, Chart A5.2 at *http://dx.doi.org/10.1787/888933115977*.

How much more do tertiary graduates earn?

- *Earnings tend to rise in line with people's level of education, in all OECD countries.*
- *Adults with university-level education in OECD countries can expect to earn 70% more than those who have only attained upper secondary education.*
- *The difference in relative earnings between younger and older workers increases with educational attainment, on average across OECD countries, benefitting more educated older workers.*
- *Men earn more than women at all levels of education in many countries, but the largest gap is among individuals with tertiary education, where women earn about 75% as much as men.*

Significance

This section examines the relative earnings of workers with different levels of education. Higher levels of education and skills usually translate into better chances of employment and higher earnings. Differences in pre-tax earnings between educational groups provide a good indication of supply and demand for education. Combined with data on earnings over time, these differences provide a strong signal of whether education systems are meeting the demands of the labour market.

Findings

Educational attainment is strongly linked to average earnings. Adults with tertiary education earn more than twice as much as adults with upper secondary education in Brazil, Chile and Hungary. At the other end of the education scale, individuals without upper secondary education face large earnings disadvantages in all countries. In Brazil, Turkey and the United States they earn, at best, 35% less than people with upper secondary education.

Gender gaps in earnings persist, in many countries, regardless of the levels of education and skills. The gap is smallest among those with upper secondary and post-secondary non-tertiary education, and largest among those with tertiary education. Women with tertiary education earn 80% or more of men's earnings in only four countries: Belgium, Slovenia, Spain and Turkey; in Brazil, Chile and Hungary, women who have obtained a tertiary degree earn 65% or less of what tertiary-educated men earn.

The earnings advantage from education increases with age in most OECD countries; relative earnings for tertiary-educated 55-64 year-olds are up to 35 percentage points higher than those of 25-34 year-olds with tertiary education on average. At the other end of the scale, the earnings disadvantage for those with below upper secondary education increases with age in all countries except Denmark, Finland, Germany, Norway, the Slovak Republic, Sweden and the United Kingdom.

Age also narrows the gender gap in wages for women with an upper secondary education. Women aged 55-64 with this education level can expect to earn about 80% as much as their male peers.

Trends

Between 2005 and 2012, the relative earnings of adults without upper secondary education either remained stable or fell in countries with available data. In addition, in most of these countries, relative earnings for tertiary-educated adults increased or remained stable; the only exceptions are Hungary and the United States. These differences suggest that the demand for higher-level and updated skills has grown, and that individuals with lower levels of skills are even more vulnerable today.

Definitions

Relative earnings are percentages of the earnings of adults with levels of education other than upper secondary relative to the earnings of those with upper secondary education.

Earnings data differ across countries in a number of ways, including whether they are reported annually, monthly or weekly. Thus results shown here should be interpreted with caution. For some countries, data on full-time, full-year earnings are based on the European Survey on Income and Living Conditions (EU-SILC), which uses a self-designated approach in establishing full-time status.

Information on data for Israel:
http://dx.doi.org/10.1787/888932315602.

Going further

For additional material, notes and a full explanation of sourcing and methodologies, see *Education at a Glance 2014* (Indicator A6).

Areas covered include:

- Trends in relative earnings of the population.
- Differences in earnings by gender and by age.
- Differences in earnings distribution according to educational attainment.

Further reading from OECD

OECD (2012), *Better Skills, Better Jobs, Better Lives: A Strategic Approach to Skills Policies*, OECD Publishing, Paris, http://dx.doi.org/10.1787/9789264177338-en.

Figure 3.3. **Relative earnings of workers with university education or higher, by gender, 2012**

This figure compares earnings of 25-64 year-old men and women with university or advanced research level education, using upper secondary education as a baseline (the line labelled 100 in the left-hand scale on the graph).

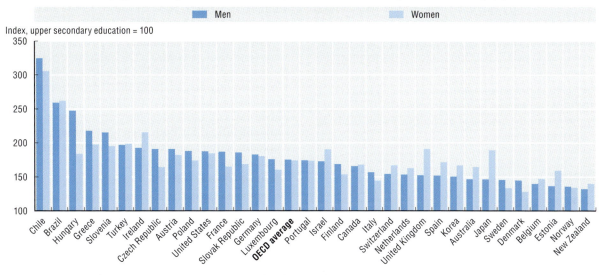

Source: OECD (2014), *Education at a Glance 2014*, Chart A6.1, available at *http://dx.doi.org/10.1787/888933116205.*

Figure 3.4. **Relative earnings of workers with below upper secondary education, by gender, 2012**

This figure compares earnings of 25-64 year-old men and women with below upper secondary education, using upper secondary education as a baseline (the line labelled 100 in the left-hand scale on the graph).

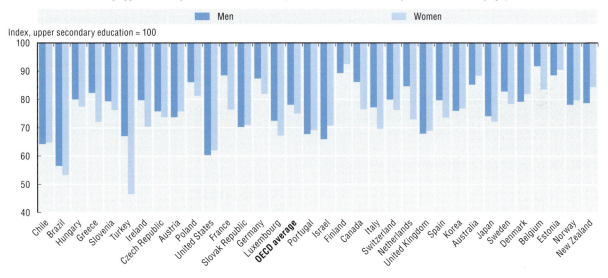

Source: OECD (2014), *Education at a Glance 2014*, Chart A6.1, available at *http://dx.doi.org/10.1787/888933116205.*

What are the incentives to invest in education?

- *People invest about USD 50 000 to obtain a tertiary degree in OECD countries, but men can expect to earn USD 350 000 more in their lifetime than those with an upper secondary or post-secondary non-tertiary education, and women USD 250 000 more.*

- *Education does not only pay off for individuals; it also contributes to the public good in the form of greater tax revenues and social contributions.*

- *The net public return on an investment in tertiary education is over USD 105 000 for men on average across OECD countries – nearly three times the amount of public investment – and over USD 60 000 for women.*

Significance

Higher educational achievement benefits both individuals and society, not only financially, but also in terms of well-being. The efforts people make to continue education after compulsory schooling can be thought of as an investment with the potential to bring rewards in the form of future financial returns. Society, in turn, profits through reduced public expenditure on social welfare programmes and revenues earned through taxes paid once individuals enter the labour market.

Findings

Rewards are typically higher for those with higher levels of education. Gross earning benefits for a person with an upper secondary or post-secondary non-tertiary degree, compared to benefits for a person who has not attained this level of education, are particularly high in Austria, the Netherlands (for a woman), Norway and the United States. They amount to at least USD 260 000 for a man and USD 160 000 for a woman.

Higher education generates gross earnings benefits, compared with the income of a person with an upper secondary or post-secondary non-tertiary education, of USD 350 000 for men and USD 250 000 for women across OECD countries.

Individuals invest about USD 50 000 to obtain a tertiary degree in OECD countries. In Japan, the Netherlands and the United States, average investment exceeds USD 100 000 when direct costs such as tuition fees and indirect costs such as loss of earnings while studying are taken into account.

With few exceptions, net private returns are higher for individuals who attain tertiary education than those without. Only in Norway and Sweden does upper secondary or post-secondary non-tertiary education bring higher returns, to men. Among those with tertiary education, net private returns are typically higher for men than for women. In Greece, New Zealand, Spain and Turkey, the returns are higher for women.

Investing in upper secondary or post-secondary non-tertiary education generates a net public return of USD 39 000 for men and USD 24 000 for women across their working life, on average across the 28 OECD countries with available data. The public benefits are twice as large as the overall public costs of upper secondary or post-secondary non-tertiary education, for both men and women. In the United Kingdom, public benefits are nine times larger than the public costs for a man with this level of education and nearly ten times larger for a woman.

On average across OECD countries, public investment in a person's tertiary education is USD 38 000 higher than that for an individual's upper secondary or post-secondary education (taking into account public direct spending and indirect costs). Public investment in an individual's tertiary education is highest in Austria, Denmark, Finland, Germany, the Netherlands, Sweden and the United States.

Definitions

The economic returns to education are measured by the net present value or NPV. In the calculations, private investment costs include after-tax foregone earnings adjusted for the probability of finding a job (unemployment rate) and direct private expenditures on education. Public costs include lost income tax receipts during the school years, and public expenditures.

Information on data for Israel:
http://dx.doi.org/10.1787/888932315602.

> ### *Going further*
>
> For additional material, notes and a full explanation of sourcing and methodologies, as well as a technical explanation of how the NPV is derived, see *Education at a Glance 2014* (Indicator A7).
>
> Areas covered include:
>
> – Private costs and benefits of education, by education level and gender.
>
> – Public costs and benefits of education, by education level and gender.

Figure 3.5. **Public return on tertiary education, by gender, 2010**

This figure shows the difference between public benefits (increased tax revenues and lower need for social transfers, among others) and public costs (direct spending and foregone tax revenues) for men and women obtaining tertiary education, as compared to those with upper secondary or post-secondary non-tertiary education.

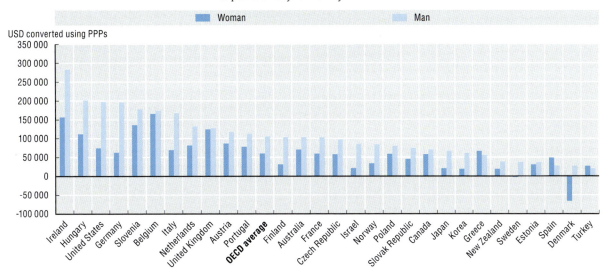

Source: OECD (2014), *Education at a Glance 2014*, Tables A7.4a and A7.4b, available at *http://dx.doi.org/10.1787/888933116414* and *http://dx.doi.org/10.1787/888933116433*.

Figure 3.6. **Private return on tertiary education, by gender, 2010**

This figure shows the difference between private benefits (increased lifetime earnings) and private costs (tuition fees and foregone earnings) for men and women who successfully complete tertiary education, as compared to those with upper secondary or post-secondary non-tertiary education.

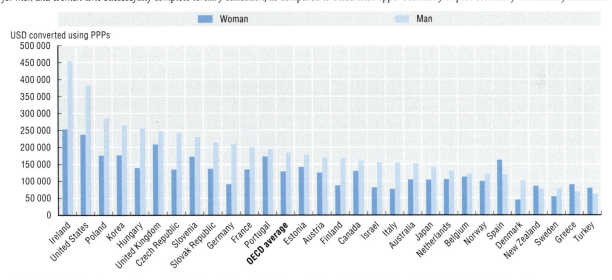

Source: OECD (2014), *Education at a Glance 2014*, Tables A7.3a and A7.3b, available at *http://dx.doi.org/10.1787/888933116376* and *http://dx.doi.org/10.1787/888933116395*.

How are student performance and equity in education related?

- *Boys outperform girls in mathematics in 37 of the 64 countries that participated in PISA 2012, and girls outperform boys in five countries.*
- *On average, 13% of students in OECD countries are top performers in mathematics and 23% are low performers in mathematics.*
- *Shanghai-China performs the highest in mathematics of all countries and economies that participated in PISA 2012 with a mean score of 613 points.*

Significance

Modern societies reward individuals not for what they know, but for what they can do with what they know. The Programme for International Student Assessment (PISA) 2012 results, which measured 15-year-olds' academic performance in 64 countries and economies around the world, examine not only whether students can reproduce what they have learned, but also how well they can apply their knowledge in unfamiliar settings. PISA results reveal what is possible in education by showing what students in the highest-performing and most rapidly improving education systems can do. An analysis of PISA in the context of various socio-economic factors shows how equitably participating countries are providing education opportunities and realising education outcomes – an indication of the level of equity in the society, as a whole.

Findings

Despite the stereotype that boys are better than girls at mathematics, boys show an advantage in only 37 out of the 64 countries and economies that participated in PISA 2012, and in only six countries is the gender gap – in favour of boys – larger than the equivalent of half a year of school. In contrast, in only five countries – Iceland, Jordan, Malaysia, Qatar and Thailand – do girls outperform boys in mathematics.

Shanghai-China performs the highest in mathematics of all countries and economies that participated in PISA 2012, with a mean score of 613 points – 119 points, or the equivalent of nearly three years of schooling, above the OECD average. The difference between the highest-scoring economy and the lowest-scoring country is 245 points. On average across OECD countries, 13% of students are top performers in mathematics and 23% are low performers.

Among OECD countries, 15% of the difference in performance among students is explained by disparities in students' socio-economic status. Even more telling, some 39 score points – the equivalent of around one year of formal schooling – separate the mathematics performance of those students who are considered socio-economically advantaged and those whose socio-economic status is close to the OECD average.

Trends

Of the 64 countries and economies with trend data between 2003 and 2012, 25 improved in mathematics performance, 25 showed no change, and 14 deteriorated. Among the countries that showed improvement between 2003 and 2012, Italy, Poland and Portugal reduced the proportion of low performers and increased the proportion of high performers.

Of the 39 countries and economies that participated in both PISA 2003 and 2012, Mexico, Turkey and Germany improved both their mathematics performance and their levels of equity in education during the period. Between 2003 and 2012, the degree to which students' socio-economic status predicted performance in mathematics decreased overall from 17% to 15%.

Definitions

Low performers in mathematics are those students who do not reach the baseline Level 2 on the PISA assessment. At Level 2, students can interpret and recognise situations in contexts that require no more than direct inference. Top performers in mathematics score at Level 5 or 6 on the PISA assessment; they are able to draw on and use information from multiple and indirect sources to solve complex problems.

Information on data for Israel:
http://dx.doi.org/10.1787/888932315602.

Going further

For additional material, notes and a full explanation of sourcing and methodologies, see *Education at a Glance 2014* (Indicator A9).

Areas covered include:

- Gender differences in mathematics performance.
- Trends on performance in mathematics.
- Relationship between performance in mathematics and socio-economic status.
- Trends on equity.

Further reading from OECD

OECD (2014), *PISA 2012 Results: What Students Know and Can Do (Volume I): Student Performance in Mathematics, Reading and Science*, PISA, OECD Publishing, Paris, *http://dx.doi.org/10.1787/9789264208780-en.*

OECD (2013), *PISA 2012 Results: Excellence through Equity (Volume II): Giving Every Student the Chance to Succeed*, PISA, OECD Publishing, Paris, *http://dx.doi.org/10.1787/9789264201132-en.*

Figure 3.7. **Student performance in mathematics, by gender, PISA 2012**

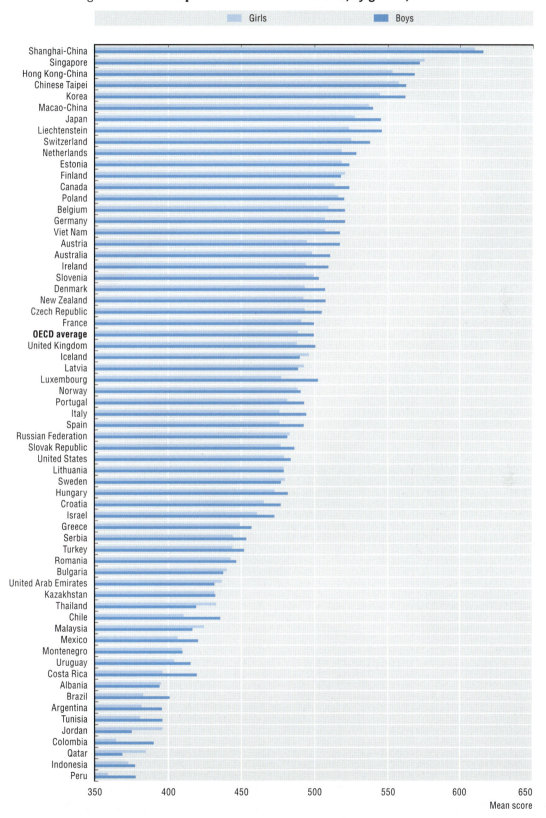

Source: OECD (2014), *Education at a Glance 2014*, Chart A9.1, available at *http://dx.doi.org/10.1787/888933116813*.

4. PAYING FOR EDUCATION

How much is spent per student?

What share of national wealth is spent on education?

How much public and private investment in education is there?

How do public and private schools differ?

How much do tertiary students pay?

What are education funds spent on?

How much is spent per student?

- *In 2011, OECD countries on average spent USD 9 487 per student each year from primary through tertiary education: USD 8 296 per primary student, USD 9 280 per secondary student and USD 13 958 per tertiary student.*
- *In primary, secondary and post-secondary non-tertiary education, 94% of total spending per student is devoted to core educational services. Greater differences are seen at the tertiary level, partly because spending on research and development (R&D) represents an average of 32% of total spending per student.*
- *Spending per student on primary, secondary and post-secondary non-university-level education increased by 17 percentage points on average among OECD countries between 2005 and 2011.*

Significance

This section shows the levels of combined public and private spending on education. Demand for high-quality education, which may mean spending more per student, must be balanced against other demands on public spending and the desire to keep taxes low. Policy makers must also balance quality improvement with expansion of access to education, especially considering that spending has not kept up with expanding enrolments in many OECD countries.

Findings

Spending per student is largely affected by teachers' salaries. Indeed, high teacher salaries and low student-teacher ratios are often the main elements raising spending in the ten countries with the highest levels of spending per student at the secondary level.

There is a strong positive relationship between spending per student and GDP per capita at the primary and secondary levels – poorer countries tend to spend less than richer ones. The relationship is weaker at the tertiary level, mainly because financing mechanisms and enrolment patterns differ more at this level.

Once R&D activities and ancillary services such as welfare services to students are excluded, spending on core educational services from primary through tertiary education in OECD countries falls from an average USD 9 487 to an average USD 8 002. This results mainly from the much lower level of spending per student at the tertiary level when peripheral activities are not taken into account.

On average, OECD countries spend around two thirds more per student at the tertiary level than at the primary level. At tertiary level, however, other services, particularly research and development activities, also constitute a large slice of spending. When these are excluded, spending per student on core educational services at the tertiary level is still, on average, 11% higher than at the primary, secondary and post-secondary non-tertiary levels.

Trends

Between 1995 and 2011 spending per primary, secondary and post-secondary non-tertiary student increased in every country with available data except Italy, by an average of more than 60% (a period of relatively stable student enrolment in most countries). The increase was relatively larger over the period 1995-2005 than over the period 2005-11, on average among OECD countries.

Since the beginning of the economic crisis in 2008, spending per primary, secondary and post-secondary non-tertiary student has continued to increase, except in Denmark, Estonia, Hungary, Iceland, Italy, the Russian Federation and Spain. Spending per tertiary student has decreased in more than a third of countries, mainly because enrolment increased faster than spending. In Iceland, Ireland, Poland and the Russian Federation, however, there was an actual decrease in spending.

Definitions

Core educational services are directly related to instruction in educational institutions, including teachers' salaries, construction and maintenance of school buildings, teaching materials, books, and administration of schools.

Data refer to the financial year 2011 and are based on the UOE data collection on education statistics administered by the OECD in 2013. Spending per student at a particular level of education is calculated by dividing the total spending by educational institutions at that level by the corresponding full-time equivalent enrolment.

Information on data for Israel:
http://dx.doi.org/10.1787/888932315602.

Going further

For additional material, notes and a full explanation of sourcing and methodologies, see *Education at a Glance 2014* (Indicator B1).

Areas covered include:

- Annual spending by educational institutions per student for all services, and compared to GDP per capita.
- Cumulative spending by educational institutions per student.

Figure 4.1. **Annual spending per student, 2011**

This figure shows how much is spent annually (from public and private sources) per student by educational institutions; these data give a sense of the cost per student of formal education.

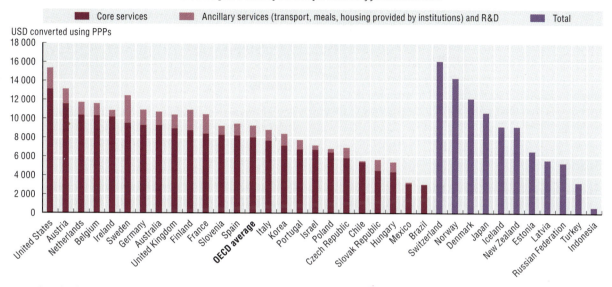

Source: OECD (2014), *Education at a Glance 2014*, Chart B1.1, available at *http://dx.doi.org/10.1787/888933117060*.

Figure 4.2. **Primary education spending in relation to other education spending, 2011**

This figure shows annual spending (by educational institutions) per student for different levels of education compared with spending at primary level.

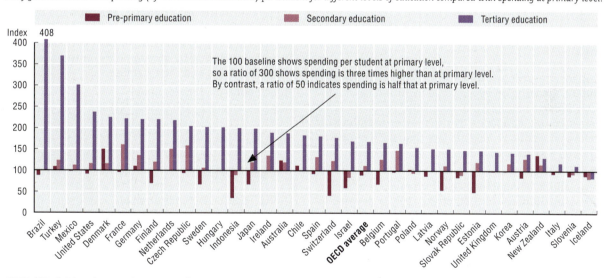

Source: OECD (2014), *Education at a Glance 2014*, Chart B1.3, available at *http://dx.doi.org/10.1787/888933117098*.

What share of national wealth is spent on education?

- *OECD countries spend 6.1% of their GDP on educational institutions on average. Seven countries (Argentina, Denmark, Iceland, Israel, Korea, New Zealand and Norway) spend more than 7%.*
- *Spending on all levels of education combined increased at a faster rate than GDP growth between 2000 and 2011 in almost all countries for which data are available.*
- *GDP rose in most countries between 2009 and 2011, but public spending on educational institutions fell in one-third of OECD countries during that time, probably as a consequence of fiscal consolidation policies.*

Significance

Countries invest in educational institutions to help foster economic growth, enhance productivity, contribute to personal and social development, and reduce social inequality. This section examines the proportion of a nation's wealth that is invested in education. The level of spending depends on how a country – including its government, private enterprises, individual students and their families – prioritises education in relation to overall spending. Education spending largely comes from public budgets and is closely scrutinised by governments. During times of financial crisis, even core sectors like education can be subject to budget cuts.

Findings

Spending on pre-primary education accounts for nearly one-tenth of spending on educational institutions, or 0.6% of GDP, on average among OECD countries. There are large differences among countries. For instance, spending on pre-primary education represents less than 0.2% of GDP in Australia and Switzerland, but about 1% or more in Denmark and Iceland.

Nearly two-thirds of combined OECD average spending on educational institutions, or 3.8% of the GDP, is devoted to primary, secondary and post-secondary non-tertiary education. Argentina and New Zealand spend 5% or more of their GDP on these levels of education, while the Czech Republic, Hungary, Japan, Latvia, the Russian Federation, the Slovak Republic and Turkey spend 3% or less.

Tertiary education accounts for one-quarter of spending on educational institutions, or 1.6% of GDP, on average across OECD countries. Canada, Chile, Korea and the United States spend between 2.4% and 2.8% of their GDP on tertiary insti-

tutions. Four countries devote 1% or less of GDP to tertiary education: Brazil, Hungary, Italy and the Slovak Republic.

Private spending on educational institutions as a percentage of GDP is highest in tertiary education, on average among OECD countries. It represents between 1.7% and 1.9% of GDP in Chile, Korea and the United States.

Trends

For all levels of education combined, public investment increased by 7% between 2008 and 2011, on average in OECD countries. However, the annual growth of public spending on educational institutions in OECD countries slowed during this period, from 4% in 2008-09 to 1% in 2009-10 and 2010-11. Over the whole period 2008-11, only Estonia, Hungary, Iceland, Italy, the Russian Federation and the United States cut public spending on educational institutions; but public spending decreased in only five countries in the period 2008-09, and in ten countries between 2009 and 2011. In Hungary, Iceland, Italy, Portugal and the Russian Federation, public spending dropped by 5% or more between 2009 and 2011.

Definitions

Data refer to the 2011 financial year and are based on the UOE data collection on education statistics administered by the OECD in 2013. Spending on educational institutions includes spending by governments, enterprises, and individual students and their families.

Information on data for Israel:
http://dx.doi.org/10.1787/888932315602.

Going further

For additional material, notes and a full explanation of sourcing and methodologies, see *Education at a Glance 2014* (Indicator B2).

Areas covered include:

- Spending on educational institutions as a percentage of GDP.
- Impact of the economic crisis on public spending on education, 2008-2011.

Figure 4.3. **Trends in education spending as a percentage of GDP (2000, 2011)**

This figure shows the share of national income that countries devote to spending on educational institutions, and how that share has changed over time.

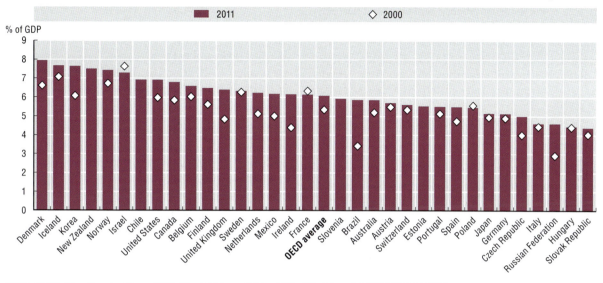

Source: OECD (2014), *Education at a Glance 2014*, Chart B2.1, available at *http://dx.doi.org/10.1787/888933117288*.

Figure 4.4. **Impact of the economic crisis on education spending, 2011**

This figure shows how the economic crisis has affected public spending on education.

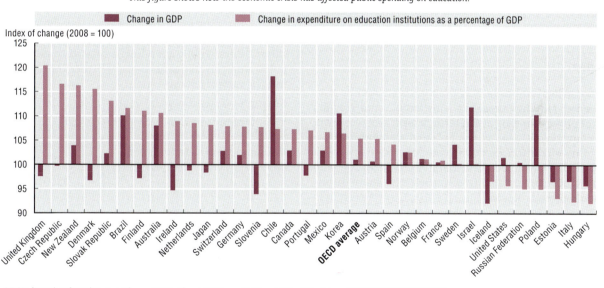

Source: OECD (2014), *Education at a Glance 2014*, Chart B2.3, available at *http://dx.doi.org/10.1787/888933117326*.

How much public and private investment in education is there?

- *Public funding accounts for 84% of all funds for educational institutions, on average in OECD countries.*
- *Nearly 92% of the funds for primary, secondary and post-secondary non-tertiary educational institutions come from public sources, on average in OECD countries.*
- *In comparison with other levels of education, tertiary institutions obtain the largest proportion of funds from private sources (31%), while pre-primary institutions obtain the second largest (19%).*

Significance

Who should support an individual's efforts to acquire more education – governments or the individuals themselves? This question is gaining importance as more people are participating in a wider range of educational programmes than ever before. In the current economic environment, many governments are finding it difficult to provide the necessary resources to support the increased demand for education in their countries through public funds alone. In addition, some policy makers assert that those who benefit the most from education – the individuals who receive it – should bear at least some of the costs. While public funding still represents a large part of countries' investment in education, the role of private sources of funding is becoming increasingly prominent.

Findings

Educational institutions in OECD countries are mainly publicly funded, although there is a substantial – and growing – level of private funding at the tertiary level. On average in OECD countries, 84% of all funds for educational institutions come directly from public sources; 16% come from private sources. However, the share of public and private funding varies widely among countries. The share of private funds exceeds 35% in Chile and Korea; by contrast, less than 3% of spending on education comes from private sources in Finland and Sweden. The countries with the lowest amounts of public spending per student in tertiary institutions are also those with the fewest students enrolled in public tertiary institutions, except Colombia, Mexico and Poland.

Individual households account for most of the private expenditure on tertiary education in most countries for which data are available. Argentina, Austria, Belgium, Canada, the Czech Republic and Sweden are the exceptions, where private expenditure from entities such as private businesses and non-profit organisations is more significant than private expenditure from households. This is mainly because tuition fees charged by tertiary institutions are low or negligible in these countries (with the exception of Canada).

Trends

Between 2000 and 2011, the average share of public funding for tertiary institutions decreased from 73.7% in 2000 to 69.1% in 2005, and then slightly to 68.3% in 2011 (on average among the 20 OECD countries for which data are available for all years). This trend is mainly influenced by some European countries, where significant changes in tuition fees took place and where enterprises participate more actively in providing grants to finance tertiary institutions. In addition, the share of private funding for tertiary education increased between 2000 and 2011 in 21 of the 26 countries for which comparable data are available, by 6 percentage points on average. During this period, the share of private funding also rose at the primary, secondary, post-secondary non-tertiary levels and at all levels of education combined, on average among OECD countries, and most significantly in the Slovak Republic and the United Kingdom (for all levels of education combined).

Definitions

Private spending includes all direct expenditure on educational institutions, whether partially covered by public subsidies or not. Public spending is related to all students at public and private institutions, whether these institutions receive public funding or not.

Data refer to the financial year 2011 and are based on the UOE data collection on education statistics administered by the OECD in 2013.

Information on data for Israel:
http://dx.doi.org/10.1787/888932315602.

Going further

For additional material, notes and a full explanation of sourcing and methodologies, see *Education at a Glance 2014* (Indicator B3).

Areas covered include:

- Distribution of public and private spending on educational institutions.
- Change in private expenditure on tertiary educational institutions, 2000-2011.

4. PAYING FOR EDUCATION

How much public and private investment in education is there?

Figure 4.5. **Share of private spending on educational institutions, 2011**

This figure shows the share of private spending on educational institutions as a percentage of total spending on educational institutions.

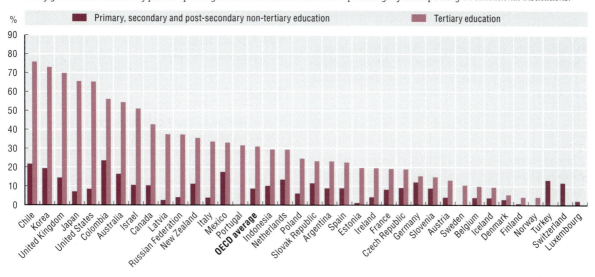

Source: OECD (2014), *Education at a Glance 2014*, Chart B3.1, available at *http://dx.doi.org/10.1787/888933117478*.

Figure 4.6. **Distribution of spending on tertiary education, 2011**

This figure shows the distribution of public and private spending on tertiary educational institutions in 2011.

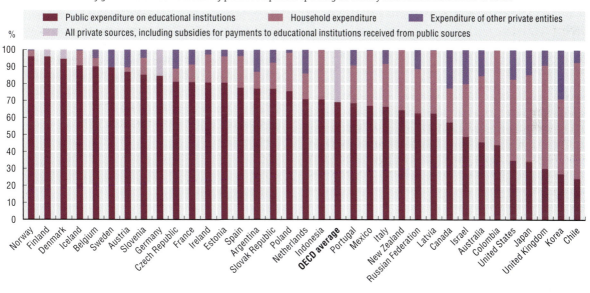

Source: OECD (2014), *Education at a Glance 2014*, Chart B3.2, available at *http://dx.doi.org/10.1787/888933117497*.

How do public and private schools differ?

- *Only about 3% of all primary and secondary students attended independent private schools in 2012.*
- *Some 11% of pupils in pre-primary education are enrolled in independent private schools.*
- *Students who attend private schools tend to perform significantly better than students who attend public schools; but students, from public or private schools, in a similar socio-economic context tend to do equally well.*

Significance

At some point in their child's education, many parents have considered whether it would be worth the expense to enrol their child in a private school. For parents or students, private schools may offer particular kinds of instruction and curricula that are not available in public schools. At the same time, private schools may segregate students and reinforce inequities in educational opportunities. Greater financial resources may enable these schools to attract and recruit the best students and teachers; however, there is no clear evidence about the relationship between the prevalence of private schools and the academic performance of education systems.

Findings

Only about 3% of all primary and secondary students attended independent private schools in 2012 in OECD countries. However, as the level of education rises, so does enrolment in independent private schools. About 2% of primary pupils are enrolled in independent private schools while 3% of lower secondary and 5% of upper secondary students are. In Brazil, Colombia, Indonesia, Japan, Mexico, Poland and Portugal, more than 10% of upper secondary students attend such schools. Meanwhile, the proportion of pre-primary students enrolled in independent private schools is considerably larger, at 11%.

Private school students perform significantly better than public school students on the OECD Programme for International Student Assessment (PISA) in 27 out of 45 countries and economies with available data. In Qatar, the score-point difference is 108 points, the equivalent of nearly three years of schooling. Public schools perform better than private schools in only 4 of the 47 countries and economies: Chinese Taipei, Hong Kong-China, Luxembourg and Thailand. However, the average socio-economic background of private school students is higher than that of public school students in 37 countries and economies. Only in Chinese Taipei is the average socio-economic status of public school students higher than that of private school students.

Public school students with similar social backgrounds to private school students tend to do equally well on the PISA surveys. After accounting for the socio-economic status of students and schools, private schools outperform public schools in only 8 countries and economies, and public schools outperform private schools in 12 countries and economies. Thus, there is no evidence to suggest that private schools help to raise the level of performance of the school system as a whole.

Trends

The share of 15-year-olds enrolled in private schools did not increase, on average, between 2003 and 2012, but some countries saw significant shifts toward public or private schools over this period. The share of students enrolled in private institutions at the tertiary level increased significantly between 2003 and 2012 in 21 of the 29 OECD countries with available data. Enrolments in private universities increased from 23% to 25%, on average, during the period, and enrolments in private vocational tertiary institutions from 33% to 37%.

Definitions

Private schools are controlled by a non-government organisation or with a governing board not selected by a government. Independent private schools receive less than 50% of their core funding from government agencies; government-dependent private schools receive more than 50% of their core funding from government agencies. Public schools are controlled and managed by a public education authority or agency.

Information on data for Israel:
http://dx.doi.org/10.1787/888932315602.

Going further

For additional material, notes and a full explanation of sourcing and methodologies, see *Education at a Glance 2014* (Indicator C7).

Areas covered include:

- School type and mathematics performance (PISA 2012).
- The degree of autonomy in determining curricula in public and private schools.

Further reading from OECD

OECD (2012), *Public and Private Schools: How Management and Funding Relate to their Socio-economic Profile*, PISA, OECD Publishing, Paris, *http://dx.doi.org/10.1787/9789264175006-en.*

Figure 4.7. **Public school enrolment among 15-year-old students (2003, 2012)**

This figure shows the percentage of 15-year-old students who are enrolled in public schools.

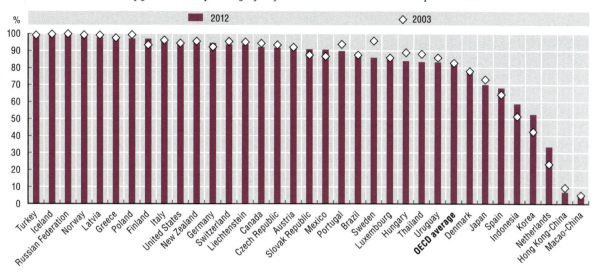

Source: OECD (2014), *Education at a Glance 2014*, Chart C7.1, available at *http://dx.doi.org/10.1787/888933119454*.

Figure 4.8. **Class size in primary schools, 2012**

This figure shows the average class size in public and private primary schools.

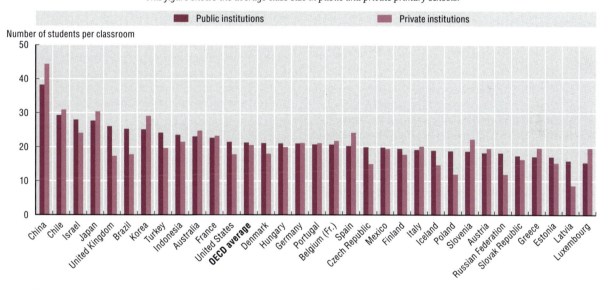

Source: OECD (2014), *Education at a Glance 2014*, Chart C7.3, available at doi *http://dx.doi.org/10.1787/888933119492*.

How much do tertiary students pay?

- *Tuition fees vary widely in OECD countries. Universities charge more than USD 1 500 in tuition fees for national students enrolled in public institutions in their own country in a third of the 26 OECD countries with available data; while in eight countries they pay nothing.*
- *Countries with high levels of tuition fees tend to be those where private entities such as companies also contribute the most to funding tertiary institutions.*
- *An increasing number of OECD countries charge higher tuition fees for international students than for national students.*
- *An average of nearly 22% of public spending on tertiary education is devoted to supporting students, households and other private entities.*

Significance

This section examines the relationships between annual tuition fees, direct and indirect public spending on education, and public subsidies for student living costs. Governments can address issues of access to and equality of education opportunities by covering part of the cost of education and related expenses, particularly for low-income students. But how this aid is given – whether through grants, scholarships or loans – is a subject of debate in many countries.

Findings

There are large differences among countries in the average tuition fees charged by university-level institutions for national students in first-degree programmes. In Denmark, Finland, Iceland, Mexico, Norway, Poland, Slovenia and Sweden, public institutions do not charge tuition fees. By contrast, tuition fees for public institutions are higher than USD 1 500 in one-third of the countries with available data, and they reach more than USD 5 000 in Chile, Japan, Korea and the United States. Tuition fees for second and further degree programmes are generally not much higher than those for first-degree programmes for public institutions and government-dependent private institutions, across OECD countries. Exceptions to this pattern are found in Australia, Chile and the United Kingdom.

Countries where students pay tuition fees but can benefit from sizeable financial support do not have below-average levels of access to university education. Highly developed financial support systems can also help explain the high entry rates into tertiary education of some countries that charge no tuition fees.

Loans with income-contingent repayment combined with means-tested grants can help to promote access to higher education and equity while sharing the costs between the state and students.

Trends

Tuition fees continue to spark lively debate, and over the past decades, there have been substantial reforms in OECD countries. Since 1995, 14 of the 25 countries with available information implemented reforms to tuition fees. These reforms were combined with a change in the level of public support available to students in all 14 countries except Iceland and the Slovak Republic.

Since 2009, further changes have been made to tuition fees and public support systems in various countries. In the United Kingdom, tuition fees doubled in 2012, as part of a government plan to stabilise university finances. In 2011, Korea increased the level of public support available to students for higher education, to expand access to and improve equity in university-level education.

Definitions

Data refer to the financial year 2011 and are based on the UOE data collection on education statistics administered by the OECD in 2012. Data on tuition fees charged by educational institutions, financial aid to students and on reforms implemented since 1995 were collected through a special survey undertaken in 2012 and refer to the academic year 2010-11. Public subsidies to households include grants/scholarships, public student loans, family or child allowances contingent on student status, public support in cash or in kind for housing, transport, medical expenses, books and supplies, social, recreational and other purposes, and interest-related subsidies for private loans.

Information on data for Israel:
http://dx.doi.org/10.1787/888932315602.

Going further

For additional material, notes and a full explanation of sourcing and methodologies, see *Education at a Glance 2014* (Indicator B5).

Areas covered include:

- Average tuition fees charged by university-level educational institutions.
- Distribution of financial aid to students.
- Governance of tertiary institutions.

Further reading from OECD

OECD Reviews of Tertiary Education (series).

Higher Education Management and Policy (journal).

Figure 4.9. **Tuition fees for university, 2011**

This figure shows the average annual tuition fees charged to full-time national students in public institutions for university-level education.

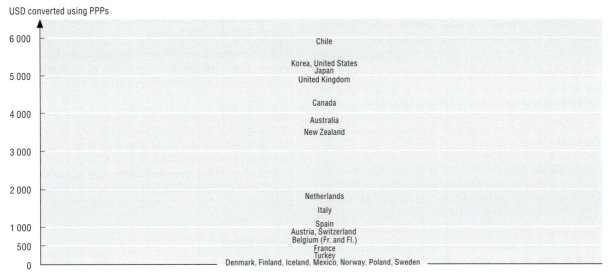

Source: OECD (2014), *Education at a Glance 2014*, Chart B5.2, available at *http://dx.doi.org/10.1787/888933117820*.

Figure 4.10. **Public support for tertiary education, 2011**

This figure shows the public support for tertiary education given to households and other private entities as a percentage of total public spending on education, broken down by the type of subsidy.

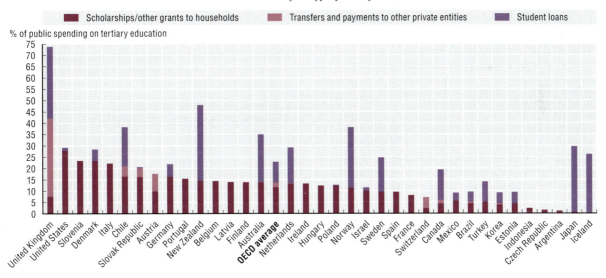

Source: OECD (2014), *Education at a Glance 2014*, Chart B5.3, available at *http://dx.doi.org/10.1787/888933117839*.

What are education funds spent on?

- *Current expenditure accounts for an average of 90% or more of total spending on education, all levels of education combined except pre-primary.*
- *Teachers' salaries account for most current expenditure in OECD and other partner countries with available data.*
- *Current expenditure other than staff costs is largest at the tertiary level, where it reaches 33% of all current expenditure, on average among OECD countries. This is partly due to the higher costs of facilities and equipment in tertiary education.*

Significance

This section details how OECD countries spend their funds for education, including the split between capital expenditure, which is one-off spending on items such as school buildings and current expenditure on items, such as teacher salaries. How spending is apportioned, both between current and capital outlays and within these categories, can affect the quality of services, the condition of facilities, and the ability of education systems to adjust to changing demographic and enrolment trends.

Findings

Current expenditure is the largest share of education spending. This is due to the labour-intensiveness of education, with teacher salaries accounting for a very large slice of current – and total – education spending. In 2011, about 90% or more of total expenditure was devoted to current expenditure at the primary, secondary and post-secondary non-tertiary levels of education combined (92.6%) and at the tertiary level (89.5%).

Staff salaries make up most of current expenditure in primary, secondary and post-secondary non-tertiary education in OECD countries, with an average of over 62% devoted to compensating teachers, 15% to other staff and 21% to expenditure other than compensation. In tertiary education, most current expenditure is also related to staff costs in all countries except the Czech Republic and Indonesia. Over 80% of current expenditure in tertiary education is devoted to compensation of staff in Brazil, Colombia and Iceland.

There are relatively large differences in how current expenditure is allocated between the primary, secondary, and post-secondary non-tertiary levels on the one hand and tertiary education on the other. The share devoted to compensation of teachers is smaller at the tertiary level in all countries except Colombia. Only six countries spend more than 30% of their current expenditure on items other than staff costs in primary, secondary and post-secondary non-tertiary education: the Czech Republic (39.9%), Denmark (31.2%), Finland (35.8%), Korea (30.9%), the Slovak Republic (34.0%) and Sweden (32.8%).

Current expenditure other than staff costs is largest at the tertiary level, where it reaches 33% of all current expenditure, on average for OECD countries. This is partly due to the higher costs of facilities and equipment in tertiary education. At the tertiary level of education, the share of total expenditure devoted to capital expenditure is higher than that for primary, secondary and post-secondary non-tertiary education combined in 25 OECD countries. This may be linked to the expansion of tertiary education in recent years, and a consequent need for new buildings to be constructed.

Definitions

Capital expenditure refers to spending on assets that last longer than one year, including construction, renovation or major repair of buildings and new or replacement equipment. Current expenditure refers to spending on goods and services consumed within the current year and requiring recurrent production in order to sustain educational services.

Data refer to the financial year 2011 and are based on UOE data collection on education statistics administered by the OECD in 2013. Calculations cover expenditure by public institutions or, where available, by both public and private institutions.

Information on data for Israel: *http://dx.doi.org/10.1787/888932315602.*

Going further

For additional material, notes and a full explanation of sourcing and methodologies, see *Education at a Glance 2014* (Indicator B6).

Areas covered include:

- Expenditure on educational institutions by service category as a percentage of GDP.
- Distribution of current expenditure on educational institutions by level of education.

Figure 4.11. **Staff costs as a percentage of current expenditure in education, 2011**

This figure shows the percentage of current expenditure devoted to paying staff in primary, secondary and post-secondary non-tertiary education. Other areas of current spending include transport, student counselling, and recurring spending on school materials and research.

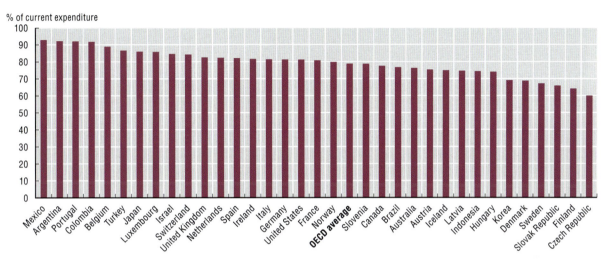

Source: OECD (2014), *Education at a Glance 2014*, Chart B6.1, available at *http://dx.doi.org/10.1787/888933117915*.

Figure 4.12. **Current and capital expenditure in tertiary education, 2011**

This figure shows the distribution of current and capital expenditure in tertiary education by country.

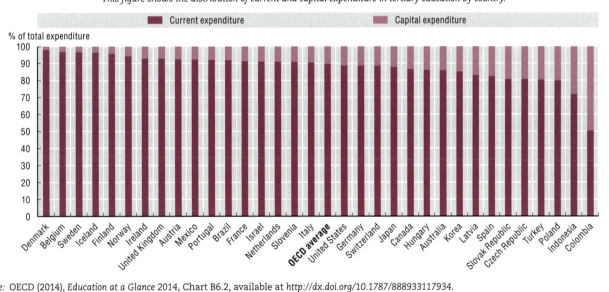

Source: OECD (2014), *Education at a Glance 2014*, Chart B6.2, available at *http://dx.doi.org/10.1787/888933117934*.

5. THE SCHOOL ENVIRONMENT

How long do students spend in the classroom?

How many students are in each classroom?

How much are teachers paid?

How much time do teachers spend teaching?

Who are the teachers?

How long do students spend in the classroom?

- *Students in OECD countries receive an average of 7 475 hours of compulsory instruction during their primary and lower secondary education.*
- *Reading, writing and literature, mathematics, and the arts account for 45% of compulsory instruction time for primary school students, on average in OECD countries, and 39% of compulsory instruction time for lower secondary school students (with instruction in first and foreign languages instead of arts).*
- *In OECD countries, an average of 4% of compulsory instruction time for primary and lower secondary students is devoted to compulsory subjects with a flexible timetable.*

Significance

This section examines the amount of time primary and lower secondary students spend in formal education. The choices that countries make about how much time should be devoted to instruction and which subjects should be compulsory reflect national and/or regional education priorities. Since a large part of public investment in education goes to instruction time in formal classroom settings, the length of time students spend in school is an important factor in determining the amount of funding that should be devoted to education.

Findings

Compulsory instruction time is dedicated to teaching the compulsory curriculum. In OECD countries, students attend an average of 4 553 hours of compulsory instruction during primary school and an average of 2 922 hours during lower secondary education. While the average total compulsory instruction time for primary and lower secondary students in OECD countries is 7 475 hours, formal instruction-time requirements range from 5 304 hours in Hungary to 10 120 hours in Australia.

The proportion of the compulsory curriculum that is devoted to reading, writing and literature varies widely among OECD and G20 countries. It ranges from 18% in Poland to 37% in France for primary students; for lower secondary students, it ranges from 12% in the Czech Republic, Finland, Ireland and Japan to 33% in Italy.

On average, the largest portion of the curriculum for primary students is devoted to reading, writing and literature but the size of that portion differs widely. For example, in Chile, Germany, Iceland, Ireland and Poland, reading, writing and literature accounts for 20% or less of compulsory instruction time while in France and Mexico, it accounts for 35% or more of compulsory instruction time. In most countries, the second largest share of time is spent studying mathematics.

At the lower secondary level, an average of 39% of the compulsory curriculum is composed of three subjects: reading, writing and literature (14%), first and other foreign languages (13%) and mathematics (12%). In 11 countries, however, instruction in foreign languages accounts for the largest share of compulsory core curriculum at the lower secondary level (in some cases combined with another subject): Belgium (Flemish Community), Finland, France, Germany, Iceland, Israel, Japan, Luxembourg, Norway, Poland and Portugal.

On average in OECD countries, 4% of compulsory instruction time is allocated to subjects chosen by schools at the primary level. At the lower secondary level, 4% of compulsory instruction time is allocated to subjects chosen by schools and another 4% to subjects chosen by the students.

Definitions

Data on teaching time are from the 2013 Joint Eurydice-OECD Instruction time data collection and refer to instruction time during compulsory primary and full time (lower and upper) secondary general education for the school year 2013-14. Previous editions of *Education at a Glance* used a different survey to collect data on instruction time; thus, this year's data are not comparable with the figures in the previous additions.

Information on data for Israel:
http://dx.doi.org/10.1787/888932315602.

Going further

For additional material, notes and a full explanation of sourcing and methodologies, see *Education at a Glance 2014* (Indicator D1).

Areas covered include:

- Compulsory and intended instruction time in public institutions.
- Instruction time per subject.

Figure 5.1. **Compulsory instruction hours in general education in public institutions, 2014**

This figure shows the hours of compulsory instruction that students receive in primary and lower secondary education.

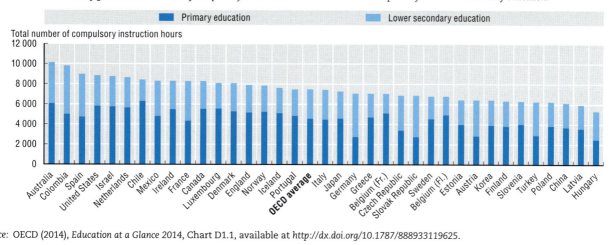

Source: OECD (2014), *Education at a Glance 2014*, Chart D1.1, available at *http://dx.doi.org/10.1787/888933119625*.

Figure 5.2. **Instruction time by subject, 2014**

These figures show the instruction time per subject as a percentage of total compulsory instruction time in primary and lower secondary education.

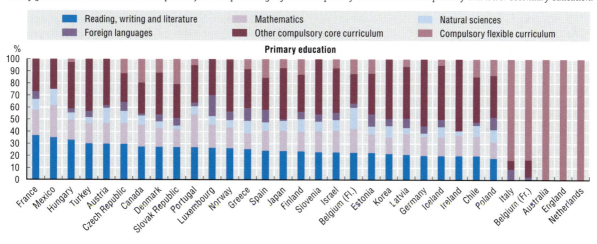

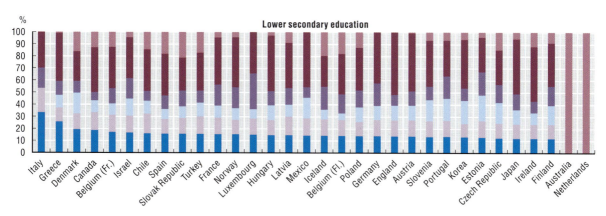

Source: OECD (2014), *Education at a Glance 2014*, Charts D1.2a and D1.2b, available at *http://dx.doi.org/10.1787/888933119644* and *http://dx.doi.org/10.1787/888933119663*.

How many students are in each classroom?

- *The average primary school class in OECD countries has 21 students, but classes are usually larger in partner countries.*
- *The number of students per class increases by two students between primary and lower secondary education, on average in OECD countries.*
- *The average class size at primary level decreased between 2000 and 2012, especially in countries that had relatively large classes, such as Korea and Turkey.*

Significance

This section examines the number of students per class at the primary and lower secondary levels, in both public and private institutions. Class size is a hotly debated topic in many OECD countries and has a considerable impact on the level of current spending on education. While smaller classes are often perceived as enabling a higher quality of education, particularly among pupils from disadvantaged backgrounds, overall, evidence of the effect of differences in class size on student performance is weak.

Findings

The average primary school class in OECD countries had 21 pupils in 2012, ranging from fewer than 16 pupils in Latvia and Luxembourg to more than 30 in Chile. China also had more than 30 pupils per class. The number of students per class tends to increase between primary and lower secondary education. In lower secondary education, the average class in OECD countries has nearly 24 students. Class size for all countries with available data range from 20 students or less in Estonia, Finland, Iceland, Latvia, Luxembourg, the Russian Federation, the Slovak Republic, Slovenia and the United Kingdom, to around 33 students per class in Japan, Korea and Indonesia, and almost 52 students in China.

The student-teacher ratio decreases in all countries with available data between the primary and lower secondary levels in all but four OECD countries: Chile, Iceland, Mexico and Norway.

Average class size generally does not differ between public and private institutions by more than two students per class, among OECD and partner countries. However, there are marked differences among countries. For example, the average primary school class at a public school is larger by four or more students than that at a private school in Brazil, the Czech Republic, Iceland, Israel, Latvia, Poland, the Russian Federation, Turkey, the United Kingdom and the United States. In contrast, the average private school class exceeds the average public school class by four or more students in Spain.

Class size varies significantly within countries. The biggest classes in primary education are in Chile and China, with 30 or more students per classroom, whereas in Estonia,

Latvia and Luxembourg classes have less than 17 students on average.

Trends

From 2000 to 2012, the average class size in countries with available data for both years decreased at both the primary and lower secondary levels, and the range of class size among OECD countries narrowed. The slight decrease in average primary class size can be partly explained by reforms on class size during that period. Primary class sizes decreased most notably (by more than four students) in countries that had relatively large class sizes in 2000, such as Korea and Turkey. However, class size has grown in some countries that had relatively small classes in 2000, most notably Denmark and Iceland.

Definitions

Class size is calculated by dividing the number of students enrolled by the number of classes. In order to ensure comparability among countries, special-needs programmes are excluded. Data refer to the 2011-12 school year, and are based on the UOE data collection on education statistics administered by the OECD in 2012.

Information on data for Israel:
http://dx.doi.org/10.1787/888932315602.

Going further

For additional material, notes and a full explanation of sourcing and methodologies, see *Education at a Glance 2014* (Indicator D2).

Areas covered include:

- Average class size, by type of institution (public, government-dependent private and independent private) and by level of education (primary, lower secondary and upper secondary).
- Ratio of students to teaching staff.
- Teaching staff and non-teaching staff (teachers' aides) employed in educational institutions.

Further reading from OECD

OECD (2014), *TALIS 2013 Results: An International Perspective on Teaching and Learning*, OECD Publishing, Paris, *http://dx.doi.org/10.1787/9789264196261-en.*

Figure 5.3. **Average class size in primary education (2000, 2012)**

This figure shows the number of students on average in primary classes.

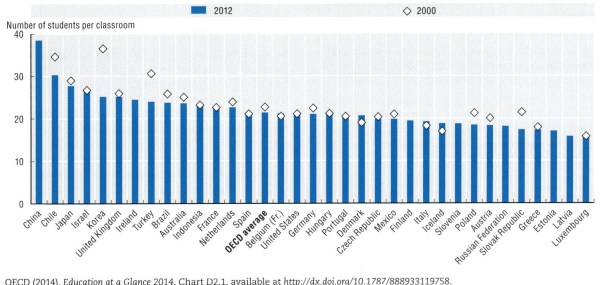

Source: OECD (2014), *Education at a Glance 2014*, Chart D2.1, available at *http://dx.doi.org/10.1787/888933119758*.

Figure 5.4. **Average class size, by level of education, 2012**

This figure shows how class sizes differ between primary and lower secondary education.

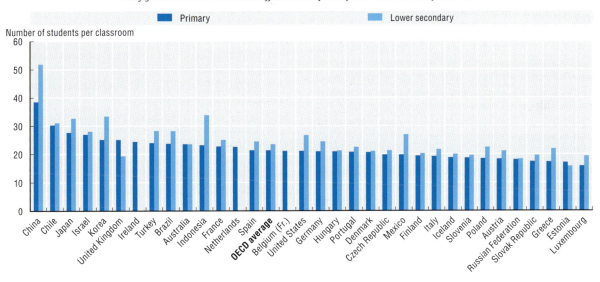

Source: OECD (2014), *Education at a Glance 2014*, Chart D2.2, available at *http://dx.doi.org/10.1787/888933119777*.

How much are teachers paid?

- *Salaries for teachers in OECD countries with at least 15 years of experience average USD 37 350 at the pre-primary level, USD 39 024 at the primary level, USD 40 570 at the lower secondary level and USD 42 861 at the upper secondary level.*
- *Teachers' salaries at primary-school level represent 85% of average earnings for 25-64 year-old full-time workers with a tertiary education, on average in OECD countries; upper secondary teachers are paid 92% of average tertiary earnings.*
- *Salaries at the top of the scale with minimum qualifications are, on average, 58% higher than starting salaries at pre-primary level and 62% higher at upper secondary level; the difference tends to be greatest when it takes many years to progress through the scale.*

Significance

This section shows the starting, mid-career and maximum statutory salaries of teachers in public pre-primary, primary and secondary education. Since teachers' salaries are the largest single cost in formal education, teacher compensation is a critical consideration for policy makers seeking to ensure both the quality of teaching and a sustainable education budget.

Findings

In most OECD countries, teachers' salaries rise with the level of education they teach. For example, in Belgium, Denmark, Finland, Indonesia, Poland and Switzerland (11 years of experience), the salary of an upper secondary teacher with at least 15 years of experience is at least 25% higher than that of a pre-primary teacher with the same amount of experience.

Teachers' salaries at the top of the scale with minimum qualifications in pre-primary education are, on average, 58% higher than starting salaries. This figure reaches 61% in primary education, 61% in lower secondary education, and 62% in upper secondary education. The difference tends to be greatest when it takes many years to progress through the scale. In countries where it takes 30 years or more to reach the top of the salary scale, salaries at the top of the scale are an average 80% higher than starting salaries.

Teachers with maximum qualifications at the top of their salary scales earn, on average, USD 48 937 at the pre-primary level, USD 50 984 at the primary level, USD 53 686 at the lower secondary level, and USD 55 119 at the upper secondary level. However, the salary premium for higher qualifications varies. Primary teachers who hold the maximum qualification earn at least 30% more than primary teachers with similar experience, but who hold the minimum qualification, in Israel, Mexico, Poland and Slovenia, for exam-

ple. However, in around one-third of countries with available data there is no difference.

Trends

Between 2000 and 2012, teachers' salaries rose, in real terms, in all countries with available data, with the exception of France, Greece and Japan. However, in most countries, salaries increased less since 2005 than between 2000 and 2005 and the economic downturn in 2008 also had a direct impact on teachers' salaries, which were either frozen or cut in some countries. As a consequence, the number of countries showing an increase in salaries, in real terms, between 2008 and 2012 shrinks to fewer than half of OECD countries.

Definitions

Teachers' salaries at different points of their career refer to the average scheduled gross salary per year for a fully qualified full-time teacher. Earnings for workers with tertiary education are average earnings for full-time, full-year workers aged between 25 and 64 year and with university-level, vocational tertiary or post-tertiary education. Data are from the 2013 OECD-INES Survey on Teachers and the Curriculum and refer to the 2011-12 school year. Data on teachers' salary at upper secondary level refer only to general programmes. Gross teachers' salaries were converted using purchasing power parities (PPPs) for private consumption from the OECD National Accounts database.

Information on data for Israel:
http://dx.doi.org/10.1787/888932315602.

Going further

For additional material, notes and a full explanation of sourcing and methodologies, see *Education at a Glance 2014* (Indicator D3).

Areas covered include:

- Teachers' salaries and trends.
- Additional payments for teachers.

Further reading from OECD

OECD (2014), *TALIS 2013 Results: An International Perspective on Teaching and Learning*, OECD Publishing, Paris, *http://dx.doi.org/10.1787/9789264196261-en.*

Figure 5.5. **Teachers' salaries in lower secondary education relative to earnings for tertiary-educated workers, 2012**

This figure compares lower secondary teachers' salaries with the earnings of other full-time workers with tertiary education.

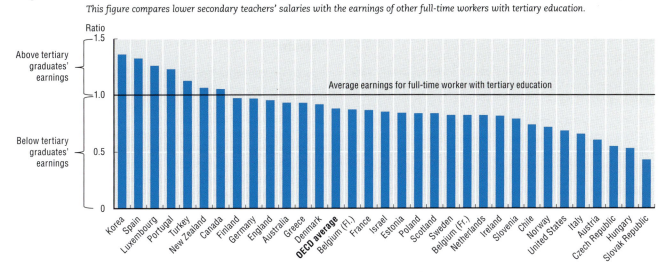

Source: OECD (2014), *Education at a Glance 2014*, Chart D3.1 available at *http://dx.doi.org/10.1787/888933119929*.

Figure 5.6. **Minimum and maximum teachers' salaries in lower secondary education, 2012**

This figure shows the gap between teachers' salaries at the start of their career, with minimum training and at the top of the scale with maximum qualification, in lower secondary education.

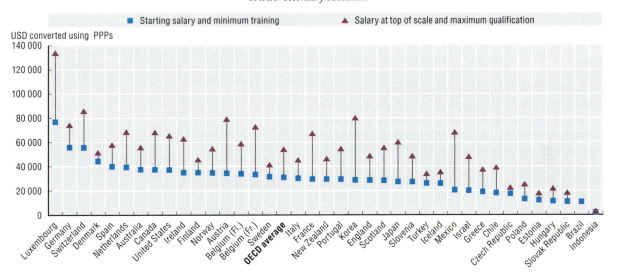

Source: OECD (2014), *Education at a Glance 2014*, Chart D3.2 available at *http://dx.doi.org/10.1787/888933119948*.

How much time do teachers spend teaching?

- *Public-school teachers teach an average of 1 001 hours per year at the pre-primary level, 782 hours at the primary level, 694 hours at the lower secondary level and 655 hours at the upper secondary level of education.*
- *The amount of teaching time increased or decreased by at least 10% between 2000 and 2012 in primary, lower secondary and/ or upper secondary education in about one third of the countries with available data.*
- *The way teachers' working time is regulated varies significantly among countries, from hours per year to number of lessons per week.*

Significance

This section examines the time teachers spend teaching and doing non-teaching work, such as preparing lessons and assessing students. Although working time and teaching time only partly determine teachers' actual workload, they do provide valuable insights into differences in what is required of teachers in different countries. Teaching hours and the extent of non-teaching duties may also affect the attractiveness of teaching as a profession. The amount of time that teachers spend teaching is also one of the factors that affect the financial resources countries need to allocate to education.

Findings

The average number of teaching hours in public pre-primary schools is 1 001 hours per year, but ranges from 532 hours in Mexico to over 1 500 hours in Iceland, Norway and Sweden. Public primary school teachers teach an average of 782 hours per year, but teaching time ranges from less than 570 hours in Greece and the Russian Federation to over 1 000 hours in Chile, Indonesia and the United States. The number of teaching hours in public lower secondary schools averages 694 hours per year, but ranges from 415 hours in Greece to over 1 000 hours in Argentina, Chile, Mexico and the United States. Teachers in public upper secondary schools teach an average of 655 hours per year, but this ranges from 369 hours in Denmark to over 1 000 hours in Argentina, Chile and the United States.

Pre-primary teachers are required to teach around 25% more hours than primary school teachers, on average; but the actual time during which teachers are required to be working at school, or their total working time, is often equivalent for these two levels of education.

Trends

Teaching time varied by at least 10% for at least one level of education between 2000 and 2012 in about one third of the countries with available data. The number of teaching hours changed dramatically in a few countries: it increased by 26% in Spain at the secondary level. In contrast, net teaching time dropped by around 20% between 2000 and 2012 in Korea at primary level and by around 10% in Mexico (lower secondary level), in the Netherlands (lower and upper secondary levels) and in Scotland (primary level).

Definitions

Statutory teaching time is defined as the scheduled number of 60-minute hours per year that a full-time teacher teaches a group or class of students as set by policy. Working time refers to the number of hours that a full-time teacher is expected to work. According to a country's formal policy, it can refer to time directly associated with teaching as well as the hours devoted to teaching-related activities, such as preparing lessons, counselling students, correcting assignments and tests, and meeting with parents and other staff. Data are from the 2013 OECD-INES Survey on Teachers and the Curriculum and refer to the 2011-12 school year.

Information on data for Israel:
http://dx.doi.org/10.1787/888932315602.

Going further

For additional material, notes and a full explanation of sourcing and methodologies, see *Education at a Glance 2014* (Indicator D4).

Areas covered include:

– Organisation of teachers' working time.
– Trends of number of teaching hours per year, by level of education.

Figure 5.7. **Annual teaching hours by education level, 2012**

This figure shows the variation in annual teaching hours for teachers in different levels of education.

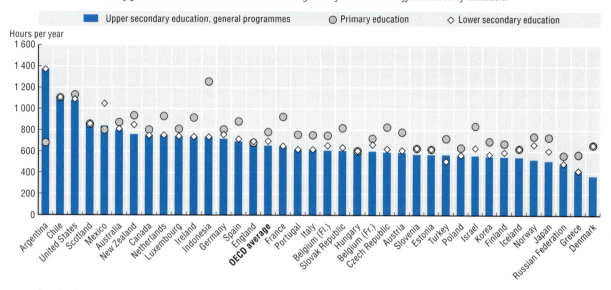

Source: OECD (2014), *Education at a Glance 2014*, Chart D4.2, available at *http://dx.doi.org/10.1787/888933120081*.

Figure 5.8. **Trends in annual teaching hours in lower secondary education (2000, 2005, 2012)**

This figure shows the trends in the number of hours teachers actually spent teaching.

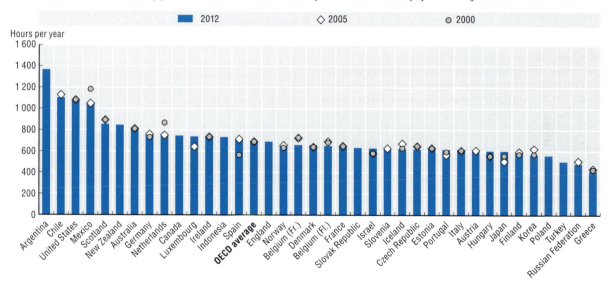

Source: OECD (2014), *Education at a Glance 2014*, Chart D4.1, available at *http://dx.doi.org/10.1787/888933120062*.

Who are the teachers?

- *About 31% of primary teachers and 36% of secondary teachers were at least 50 years old in 2012, on average in OECD countries.*
- *Two-thirds of teachers and academic staff are women on average in OECD countries, but the proportion of women among teaching staff tends to decline at higher levels of education: from 97% at the pre-primary level to 42% at the tertiary level.*
- *Lower secondary teachers have an average of 16 years of teaching experience, 10 years of it at their current school.*

Significance

This section presents a profile of the teaching workforce. Getting a better understanding of the teaching workforce means countries can anticipate teacher shortages and work to make the teaching profession a more attractive career choice. Given evidence that the quality of teachers is the most significant in-school determinant of student achievement, efforts must be made to attract top academic talent to the teaching profession and provide high-quality training.

Findings

On average across OECD countries, 31% of primary teachers are at least 50 years old. This proportion exceeds 40% in Germany, Italy and Sweden. In only six countries — Belgium, Chile, Ireland, Korea, Luxembourg and the United Kingdom — are 20% or more of primary teachers under the age of 30. The age distribution of teachers at the secondary level is roughly the same. On average among OECD countries, 36% of secondary teachers are at least 50 years old. In Austria, Estonia, Germany, Iceland, Italy, the Netherlands, New Zealand and Norway, however, the share rises to 40% or more.

Across all levels of education, women represent two-thirds of the teachers and academic staff, but the percentage of women teachers declines from each level of education to the next. For example, on average across the OECD area, women account for 97% of teachers at pre-primary level; 82% at primary level; 67% at lower secondary level; 57% at upper secondary level; and 42% in tertiary education. The share of women varies considerably between countries. For example, at lower-secondary level, the proportion of women ranges from fewer than half the teachers in Japan to more than 80% in Estonia, Iceland and the Russian Federation. Most tertiary teachers are men in all countries except Finland and the Russian Federation.

Lower secondary teachers have an average of 16 years of teaching experience, 3 years of experience in other educational roles, and 4 years of experience in other types of jobs. However, average teaching experience varies from country to country, from 20 years in Bulgaria, Estonia and Latvia to a little less than 10 years in Singapore.

Trends

Between 2002 and 2012, the proportion of secondary teachers aged 50 or older climbed by 4 percentage points on average among countries with comparable data. This increase is large (10 percentage points or more) in Italy, Japan, Korea and Portugal, and critically so in Austria, which saw a 26 percentage-point increase in this proportion during the period.

In countries that stand to lose a significant number of teachers through retirement and whose school-age population remains the same or increases, governments will have to boost the appeal of teaching to upper secondary and tertiary students, expand teacher-training programmes, and, if necessary, provide alternate routes to certification for mid-career professionals intent on changing careers.

Definitions

Data refer to the academic year 2011-12 and are based on the UOE data collection on education statistics administered by the OECD in 2012.

Information on data for Israel: *http://dx.doi.org/10.1787/888932315602.*

Going further

For additional material, notes and a full explanation of sourcing and methodologies, see *Education at a Glance 2014* (Indicator D5).

Areas covered include:

- Age and gender distribution of teachers by country and level of education.
- Change in the age distribution of teachers between 2002 and 2012.
- Teachers' work experience and employment status.

Further reading from OECD

OECD (2014), *TALIS 2013 Results: An International Perspective on Teaching and Learning*, OECD Publishing, Paris, *http://dx.doi.org/10.1787/9789264196261-en.*

Figure 5.9. **Secondary school teachers over 50 years old (2002, 2012)**

This figure shows the percentage of secondary school teachers more than 50 years old.

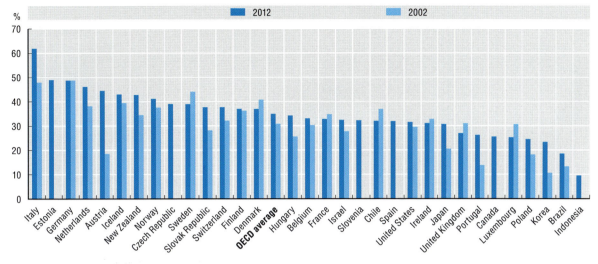

Source: OECD (2014), *Education at a Glance 2014*, Chart D5.1, available at *http://dx.doi.org/10.1787/888933120214*

Figure 5.10. **Gender distribution of teachers, 2012**

This figure shows the percentage of female teachers in primary, lower secondary and tertiary education levels.

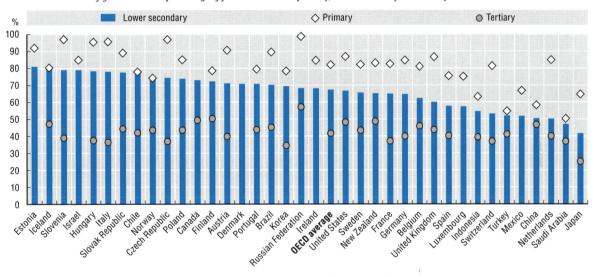

Source: OECD (2014), *Education at a Glance 2014*, Chart D5.2, available at *http://dx.doi.org/10.1787/888933120233*.

6. SPECIAL CHAPTER: SKILLS FOR LIFE

Why are adult skills important?

Why do we need computer skills?

Skills and education for society

Why do we need creative problem-solving?

The importance of financial literacy

Education and learning for adults

Why are adult skills important?

- About 87% of people with high levels of literacy have a job.
- A highly literate tertiary graduate earns, on average, about 45% more than a similarly educated adult with a low literacy level.
- More than 20% of adults whose parents have a tertiary education are highly literate.
- The proportion of younger adults who are highly literate is, on average, about 10 percentage points higher than that of older adults in OECD countries.

Significance

The way we live and work has changed profoundly – and so has the set of skills we need to participate fully in and benefit from our hyper-connected societies and increasingly knowledge-based economies. Governments need a clear picture not only of how labour markets and economies are changing, but also of the extent to which their citizens are acquiring the skills needed in the 21st century. This is particularly important for people with low skill levels as they face a much greater risk of poverty, unemployment and poor health. The Survey of Adult Skills, a product of the OECD Programme for the International Assessment of Adult Competencies (PIAAC), looks at the availability of some of these key skills in society and how they are used at work and at home. It covers 24 countries, and measures literacy, numeracy and proficiency in problem solving in technology-rich environments.

This section draws on the Survey of Adult Skills and other OECD data to show how well the supply of people with certain education qualifications and basic skills matches the demands of the labour market.

Findings

In all countries, the proportion of adults with a high level of skills is largest for tertiary-educated adults. In Australia, Finland, Japan, the Netherlands and Sweden, more than 30% of tertiary-educated adults are highly literate. Parents' education also has an effect on adult skills; on average, most highly literate people have at least one parent with tertiary education. At the other end of the scale, only about 5% of adults whose parents did not complete upper secondary education are highly literate.

Younger adults are, on average, more literate than older adults. In Finland, Japan and the Netherlands the difference between the proportion of highly literate younger adults and the proportion of older adults with the same literacy level is over 20 percentage points.

Higher skill levels are associated with higher employment rates in almost all countries where information is available. In Estonia, Flanders (Belgium), Germany, the Netherlands,

Norway and Sweden, at least 90% of high-skilled people are employed. The Survey of Adult Skills also shows that people with lower skill levels are more likely to be jobless. However, in most countries there is still a large pool of skilled adults that is not being tapped.

Highly skilled people also tend to earn more than others with the same education level. On average, highly literate people earn about 65% more than people with a low level of literacy, for all levels of education. This varies among countries, with differences in returns ranging from less than 50% in Denmark, Finland, Italy, the Russian Federation and Sweden, to over 100% in the United States.

Definitions

High levels in adult skills refer to people scoring at Level 4 or 5 in the PIAAC assessment. Low levels in adult skills refer to people scoring at Level 1 or below. See OECD (2013), *OECD Skills Outlook 2013: First Results from the Survey of Adult Skills*, OECD Publishing, Paris, *http://dx.doi.org/10.1787/9789264204256-en* for more information.

Data on population, educational attainment and labour-market status for most countries are taken from OECD and Eurostat databases, which are compiled from National Labour Force Surveys. Data on earnings are taken from a special data collection carried out by the OECD LSO Network on the earnings of those working full time and full year. Data on skill proficiency levels and mean scores are based on the Survey of Adult Skills (PIAAC) 2012.

Information on data for Israel:
http://dx.doi.org/10.1787/888932315602.

Going further

For additional material, notes and a full explanation of sourcing and methodologies, see *Education at a Glance 2014* (Indicators A1, A4, A5, A6).

Areas covered include:

- Adult skills by educational attainment.
- Labour market outcomes, and literacy and numeracy skills.
- Earnings and literacy skills.

Further reading from OECD

OECD Skills Studies (series).

Figure 6.1. **Percentage of younger and older adults with high literacy levels, 2012**

This figure shows the percentage of 25-34 and 55-64 year-olds who perform at the highest literacy levels.

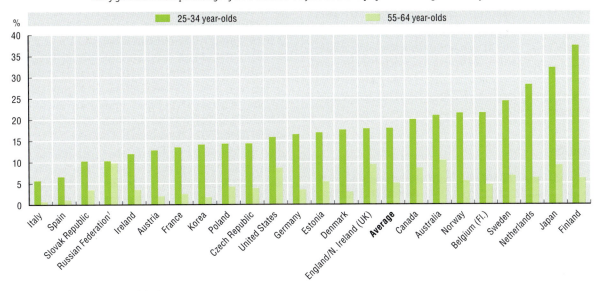

1. Data do not include Moscow municipal area.
Source: OECD (2014), *Education at a Glance 2014*, Chart A1.6, available at *http://dx.doi.org/10.1787/888933115046.*

Figure 6.2. **Employment rate of 25-64 year-olds, by literacy level, 2012**

This figure shows the percentage of 25-64 year-olds with high literacy levels who have a job compared to those with low literacy levels.

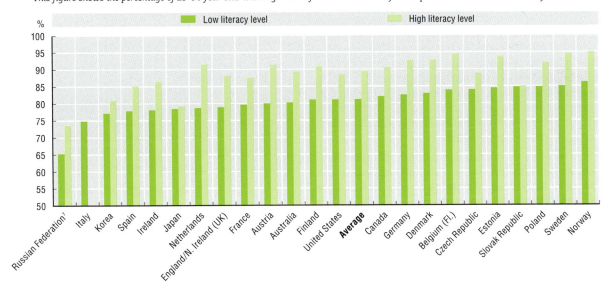

1. Data do not include Moscow municipal area.
Source: OECD (2014), *Education at a Glance 2014*, Chart A5.4, available at *http://dx.doi.org/10.1787/888933116015.*

Why do we need computer skills?

- *About a third of people in OECD countries have good computer skills.*
- *About one in ten people still lack the basic computer skills needed to for many everyday tasks.*
- *Younger adults are better at using computers than older adults, with 51% of people aged 16-24 having a high level of computer skills.*
- *On average, 36% of men are computer savvy, compared with 32% of women.*

Significance

Access to, and use of, computers both at home and at work is now widespread in OECD countries. For most of today's workers, information and communication technologies (ICT) skills are key to getting a job or a better salary, and for economies, they are crucial for remaining competitive in the global market. OECD countries anticipate that technology will continue to be a key driver of job creation, and have placed the development of ICT skills as the most important policy strategy for economic recovery. This section looks at how far adults are able to solve problems using computer technology.

Findings

About 70% of households in most OECD countries have computers and are connected to the Internet, but this does not tell us whether people are able to use their computers to acquire information, or perform practical tasks. In fact, a large number of adults still have little or no experience in using computers and most of those who do use them are only capable of using familiar basic functions such as sorting e-mails into pre-existing folders.

On average in 24 OECD countries, 9% of adults report having no prior computer experience. This ranges from around 2% in Sweden, Norway and Denmark to over 20% in Italy and the Slovak Republic. About 33% of people have good computer skills, with only 5.8% of people at the highest level and 28.2% at the level just below. In Sweden, Finland and Japan 8% of people reach the highest level.

Strikingly, the majority of workers in all countries do not have good computer skills, with up to 66% of workers in Korea, and 59% in the Slovak Republic and the United States having low ICT skills. However, about 50% of adults in skilled jobs are also highly skilled in computers, whereas only 20% of adults in elementary occupations have these skills.

Highly-educated adults are better at ICT than less-educated adults, with 52% of tertiary graduates possessing good computer skills compared to 19% of people with upper secondary education. This is also true for adults with at least one tertiary-educated parent. About 55% of them are computer savvy, compared to only 16% of adults with less-educated parents.

On average, 51% of young adults are highly-skilled in ICT. This varies from 63% in Korea, and 62% in Finland and Sweden to 38% in Poland and the United States. Very few older adults, aged 55-65, have high ICT skills.

In all the countries surveyed, men are better at using computers than women, with 4 percentage points separating the proportion of highly-skilled men and women. In Japan, this difference goes up to 11 percentage points, whereas in Australia and Canada only 1 point separates them. However, the gender gap in computer use has narrowed, particularly among younger people, with almost no differences in use between men and women aged 16-24.

Definitions

All data are based on the Survey of Adult Skills (PIAAC) 2012.

Information on data for Israel: *http://dx.doi.org/10.1787/888932315602.*

Going further

For additional material, notes and a full explanation of sourcing and methodologies, see *Education at a Glance 2014* (Box A1.2) and *OECD Skills Outlook 2013: First Results from the Survey of Adult Skills.*

Areas covered include:

- Computer skills by age, gender, education and social background.

Further reading from OECD

OECD (2013), *OECD Skills Outlook 2013: First Results from the Survey of Adult Skills,* OECD Publishing, Paris, *http://dx.doi.org/10.1787/9789264204256-en.*

OECD Reviews of Vocational Education and Training (series).

OECD Skills Studies (series).

Figure 6.3. **Adult computer and problem-solving skills, 2012**

This figure shows the percentage of 16-65 year-olds that can use computers to acquire information and resolve problems.

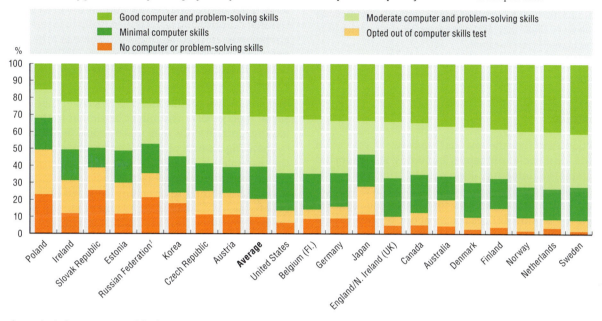

1. Data do not include Moscow municipal area.

Source: OECD (2014), *Education at a Glance 2014*, Chart Box A1.2a, available at *http://dx.doi.org/10.1787/888933115065.*

Figure 6.4. **Computer skills among men and women, 2012**

This figure shows the percentage of men and women that can use computers to acquire information and resolve problems.

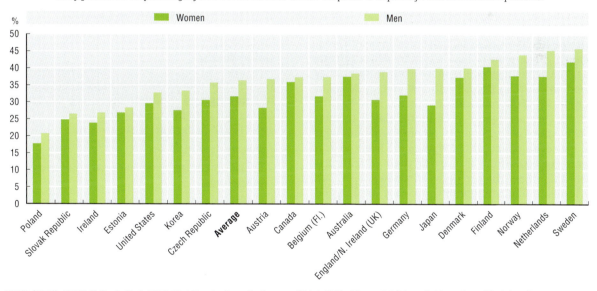

Source: OECD (2013), *OECD Skills Outlook 2013: First Results from the Survey of Adult Skills*, Figure 3.5 (P) available at *http://dx.doi.org/10.1787/888932900897.*

Skills and education for society

- *Highly literate tertiary graduates in OECD countries are more likely to believe they have a say in their government.*
- *Adults who are highly literate or have a tertiary education are more likely to think they are in good health than adults with low literacy levels or education.*
- *By improving skills women are likely to benefit more, in terms of health and trusting others, than men.*

Significance

This section examines the relationship between education and skills, and social outcomes including self-reported health status, volunteering, interpersonal trust and political efficacy. Improving health, and social and civic engagement are key policy objectives for all OECD countries. Although the significant resources spent on healthcare have generally helped people live longer, the nature of health problems has changed, with recent increases in chronic debilitating conditions such as heart disease and depression. Efforts to combat these trends depend in part on altering individuals' lifestyle choices by improving their cognitive and socio-emotional skills through education. Education may also play an important role in ensuring social cohesion by fostering the skills and resilience that underlie social and civic engagement.

Findings

Both educational attainment and literacy are strongly associated with higher levels of social outcomes. In health, people who are highly literate or have a tertiary education are, on average, 23 percentage points more likely to think they are in good health than people with low literacy levels or education, in 22 OECD countries. In Poland, how healthy people think they are seems to be more related to their level of education, with 38 points separating adults with high and low levels of education. Women are likely to gain more health benefits from improving their educational attainment than men. The gap between women with high and low levels of education who think they are in good health is 25 percentage points, compared to 22 points for men.

Education and skills are also associated with whether or not people volunteer. Although it is still unclear why this is, one reason could be that such skills motivate people to volunteer by instilling a sense that they have something to offer. Highly literate people are 11 percentage points more likely to volunteer than people with a low literacy level, on average among countries. There is particularly strong relationship between literacy and volunteering among adults without upper secondary education, as people with low levels of literacy are 8 percentage points less likely to volunteer than those with high levels of literacy, on average in 21 OECD countries.

On average, highly literate adults are 17 percentage points more likely to trust others than those with a low literacy level. This figure reaches 29 points in Norway and 33 in Denmark. Improving skills is also likely to foster more trust among women than among men. There is a 19 percentage point gap between highly and poorly skilled women who believe they can trust others, whereas for men the gap is 15 points.

The link between skills and people's belief that they have a say in their government might be similar to that for volunteering. Certain skills may make people feel more powerful by instilling a sense of control and making people feel that they can make a difference. In addition, skills are needed to understand the political issues facing a country. There is particularly strong relationship between literacy and the belief you have a say in government among people with tertiary education. Tertiary graduates with low levels of literacy are, on average, 21 percentage points less likely to believe they have a say than those with high levels of literacy, among 22 OECD countries.

Definitions

All data are based on the Survey of Adult Skills (PIAAC) 2012.

Information on data for Israel: http://dx.doi.org/10.1787/888932315602.

Going further

For additional material, notes and a full explanation of sourcing and methodologies, see *Education at a Glance 2014* (Indicator A8) and *OECD Skills Outlook 2013: First Results from the Survey of Adult Skills*.

Areas covered include:

- Social outcomes by educational attainment and literacy levels.
- Self-reported health and interpersonal trust by skill levels and gender.

Further reading from OECD

OECD (2013), *OECD Skills Outlook 2013: First Results from the Survey of Adult Skills*, OECD Publishing, Paris,
http://dx.doi.org/10.1787/9789264204256-en.

OECD (2010), *Improving Health and Social Cohesion through Education*, Educational Research and Innovation, OECD Publishing, Paris,
http://dx.doi.org/10.1787/9789264086319-en.

OECD Skills Studies (series).

Figure 6.5. **Self-reported health by literacy level, 2012**

This figure shows the percentage of highly-literate 25-64 year-olds who said they are in good health compared to those with low levels of literacy.

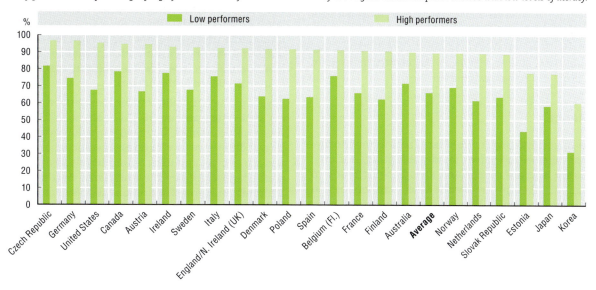

Source: OECD (2014), *Education at a Glance 2014*, Chart A8.2, available at *http://dx.doi.org/10.1787/888933116661*.

Figure 6.6. **Self-reported political influence by literacy level, 2012**

This figure shows the percentage of highly-literate 25-64 year-olds who believe they have a say in government compared to those with low levels of literacy.

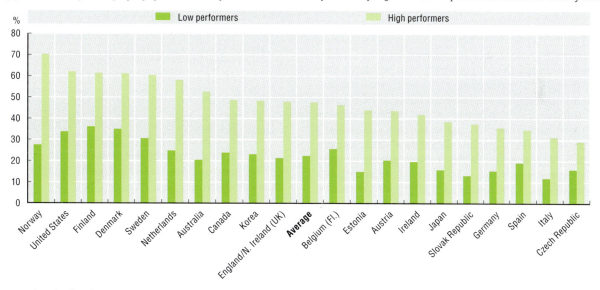

Source: OECD (2014), *Education at a Glance 2014*, Chart A8.5, available at *http://dx.doi.org/10.1787/888933116718*.

Why do we need creative problem-solving?

- *Some 11.4% of 15-year-old students in OECD countries are top performers in problem-solving.*
- *About one in five students is able to solve only straightforward problems –if any – provided that they refer to familiar situations.*
- *Boys outperform girls in problem solving in more than half of the countries and economies surveyed.*

Significance

Changes in society, the environment, and in technology mean that knowledge evolves rapidly. Adapting, learning, daring to try out new things and always being ready to learn from mistakes are among the keys to resilience and success in an unpredictable world. Few workers today, whether in manual or knowledge-based occupations, use repetitive actions to perform their job tasks, and one in ten is confronted every day with more complex problems that require at least 30 minutes to solve. Complex problem-solving skills are particularly in demand in fast-growing, highly skilled managerial, professional and technical occupations. This section presents the findings of the PISA 2012 assessment on problem solving, administered in 44 countries and economies.

Findings

A top-performing student in problem solving can devise multi-step solutions to complete complex problems efficiently. Among OECD countries, 11.4% of 15-year-old students are top performers in problem solving. In Singapore, Korea and Japan, more than one in five students achieve this high level and more than one in six students in Hong Kong-China, Chinese Taipei and Shanghai-China, Canada and Australia. However, about one in five students living in an OECD country is only able to solve straightforward problems, provided that they refer to familiar situations. In Montenegro, Malaysia, Colombia, Uruguay, Bulgaria and Brazil less than 2% of students are top-performers.

Students in East Asia obtain the highest scores in problem solving, ranging from 562 points in Singapore to 534 points in Chinese Taipei. In the OECD, 12 countries score above the average, with Canada attaining a high of 526 points. Although East Asian countries score the highest, students in Australia, Brazil, Italy, Japan, Korea, Macao-China, Serbia, England (United Kingdom) and the United States perform significantly better in problem solving, on average, than students in other countries who have similar levels in mathematics, reading and science.

Many of the best-performing countries and economies in problem solving perform well on tasks related to acquiring knowledge (such as "exploring and understanding" and "representing and formulating" tasks), and relatively low on tasks involving only the use of knowledge and that do not require substantial understanding or representation of the problem situation. Meanwhile, students in Brazil, Ireland, Korea and the United States perform strongest on interactive problems (those that require the student to uncover some of the information needed to solve the problem) compared to static problems (those that have all information disclosed at the outset).

Boys score seven points higher than girls in problem solving, on average among OECD countries. In 23 of the countries and economies surveyed, boys outperform girls. The largest differences are in Colombia, Shanghai-China, Brazil and the Slovak Republic, where boys score more than 20 points higher. Among the exceptions are the United Arab Emirates, Bulgaria, Finland and Montenegro, where girls outperform boys, on average. In 16 countries and economies, there is no significant difference in average performance in problem-solving between boys and girls.

Definitions

Results are based on student assessments administered as part of the PISA 2012 round undertaken by the OECD. The term students refers to 15-year-olds enrolled in an educational institution at secondary level, regardless of the grade level, type of institution or whether they attended school full-time or part-time.

Information on data for Israel:
http://dx.doi.org/10.1787/888932315602.

Going further

For additional material, notes and a full explanation of sourcing and methodologies see *PISA 2012 Results: Creative Problem Solving (Volume V)*.

Areas covered include:

- Distribution of student performance in creative problem solving.
- Mean score and gender differences in student performances.

Further reading from OECD

OECD (2014), *PISA 2012 Results: Creative Problem Solving (Volume V): Students' Skills in Tackling Real-Life Problems*, PISA, OECD Publishing, Paris,
http://dx.doi.org/10.1787/9789264208070-en.

Strong Performers and Successful Reformers in Education (series)

Figure 6.7. **Proficiency in problem-solving, 2012**

These figures show the average scores of students in the PISA test on problem-solving.

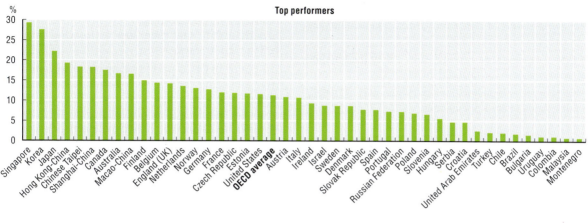

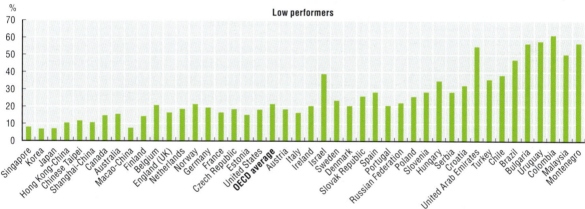

Source: OECD (2014), *PISA 2012 Results: Creative Problem Solving (Volume V)*, Figure V.2.4., available at *http://dx.doi.org/10.1787/888933003573.*

Figure 6.8. **Gender differences in problem-solving, 2012**

This figure shows the average scores of boys and girls in the PISA test on problem-solving.

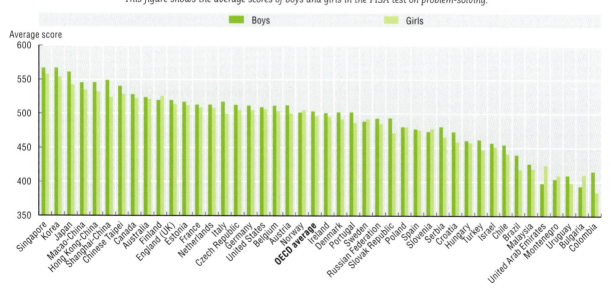

Source: OECD (2014), *PISA 2012 Results: Creative Problem Solving (Volume V)*, Figure V.4.4, available at *http://dx.doi.org/10.1787/888933003611.*

The importance of financial literacy

- *Strong performance in mathematics and reading do not necessarily mean strong literacy skills.*
- *Only one in ten students across participating OECD countries and economies is able to tackle the hardest financial literacy tasks.*
- *About 15% of students, on average, score below the baseline level of performance in the financial literacy scale.*
- *Gender gaps in financial literacy among 15-year-olds are small, unlike those found in adult populations.*

Significance

Financial literacy is an essential life skill, and high on the policy agenda in some countries. Shrinking welfare systems, shifting demographics, and the increased sophistication and expansion of financial services have all contributed to a greater awareness of the importance of ensuring that citizens and consumers of all ages are financially literate. This section looks at how far students have the knowledge and skills essential to make financial decisions and plans for their future, using the results of the PISA 2012 financial literacy assessment, which covers 13 OECD countries, and five partner economies and countries.

Findings

Finance is a part of everyday life for many 15-year-olds: they are already consumers of financial services such as bank accounts with access to online payment facilities and pre-paid mobile phones. Yet only one in ten students can tackle the hardest financial literacy tasks such as analysing financial products or calculating the balance in a bank statement while accounting for transfer fees. About 15% of students on average, score below the baseline level of performance and at best can make simple decisions about everyday spending. Shanghai-China has the highest scores in financial literacy, followed by Flanders (Belgium), Estonia, Australia, New Zealand, the Czech Republic and Poland.

There are wide differences in average performance between the highest- and lowest-performing countries and economies, but only a small proportion (16%) of the variation among countries' mean financial literacy scores is explained by per capita GDP. Among OECD countries a more socio-economically advantaged student scores 41 points higher in financial literacy than a less-advantaged student.

There are no differences in financial literacy scores between boys and girls in most countries covered by the PISA study, except Italy where boys score higher. In OECD countries and economies, there are more top-performing boys than girls, and more low-performing boys than girls, in financial literacy.

In 9 out of 13 OECD participating countries and economies, after adjusting for socio-economic status, students who hold a bank account perform as well as those who do not, while in Flanders (Belgium), Estonia, New Zealand and Slovenia, students who hold a bank account score higher in financial literacy than students of similar socio-economic status who do not. More than 70% of 15-year-olds in Australia, Flanders (Belgium), Estonia, France, New Zealand and Slovenia have a bank account, but in Israel, Poland and the Slovak Republic, fewer than 30% do.

Definitions

Data are from *PISA 2012 Results: Students and Money (Volume VI): Financial Literacy Skills for the 21st Century*.

Information on data for Israel: *http://dx.doi.org/10.1787/888932315602.*

Going further

For additional material, notes and a full explanation of sourcing and methodologies, see *PISA 2012 Results: Students and Money (Volume VI)*.

Areas covered include:

- Financial literacy skills.
- Links between literacy and numeracy skills.
- Earnings and financial literacy skills.

Further reading from OECD

OECD (2014), *PISA 2012 Results: Students and Money (Volume VI): Financial Literacy Skills for the 21st Century*, PISA, OECD Publishing, Paris,
http://dx.doi.org/10.1787/9789264208094-en.

OECD (2014), *Financial Education for Youth: The Role of Schools*, OECD Publishing, Paris,
http://dx.doi.org/10.1787/9789264174825-en.

Figure 6.9. **Financial literacy scores, 2012**

This figure shows the average score in the PISA financial literacy test among participating countries and economies.

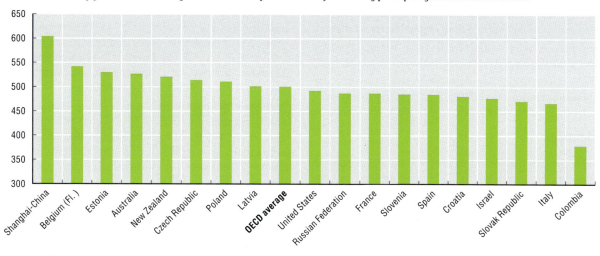

Source: OECD (2014), PISA 2012 Results: Students and Money (Volume VI), Table VI.A, available at *http://dx.doi.org/10.1787/888933094944*.

Figure 6.10. **Financial literacy levels by gender, 2012**

This figure shows the average percentage of boys and girls at each level of financial literacy proficiency in 13 OECD countries.

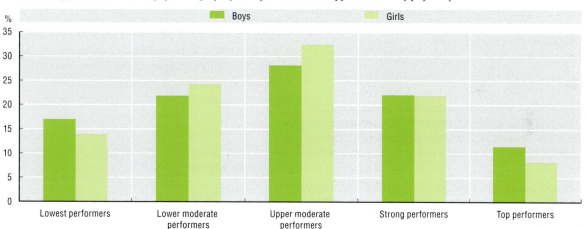

Source: OECD (2014), PISA 2012 Results: Students and Money (Volume VI), Figure VI.3.3., available at *http://dx.doi.org/10.1787/888933094906*.

Education and learning for adults

- *More than 50% of adults participate in adult education in a given year, among countries with available data.*
- *On average, 30% of adults with low literacy levels participate in adult education, compared to 74% of highly-literate adults.*
- *Participation in adult education is most common among younger adults and declines steadily among older adults.*
- *For teachers, professional development is compulsory at every level in about three-quarters of OECD and partner countries.*

Significance

Adult learning can play an important role in helping adults to develop and maintain key skills, as well as acquire new knowledge and skills, throughout life. It is crucial to provide, and ensure access to, organised learning opportunities for adults beyond initial formal education, especially for workers who need to adapt to changes throughout their careers. Lifelong learning can also contribute to non-economic goals, such as personal fulfilment, improved health, civic participation and social inclusion. This section looks at the participation levels of adults in formal and non-formal education, using the Survey of Adult Skills, which covers 24 countries. There is a clear relationship between participation in organised adult learning and the average level of key skills in a given country.

Findings

Some 51% of 25-64 year-olds participated in adult education in the previous year, on average. This ranges from above 60% in Denmark, Finland, the Netherlands, Norway and Sweden to below 25%, in Italy and the Russian Federation.

Participation in adult education in all countries is strongly related to skill level and educational attainment. A highly-literate adult is almost 2.5 times more likely to participate in education than an adult with a low level of literacy. This difference is even greater when including education, as a highly-literate tertiary graduate is almost 4 times more likely to take part in adult education than a low-educated, low-literate adult. Participation rates are also affected by parents' education, with 68% of adults with at least one tertiary-educated parent taking part in adult learning, compared with 40% of adults with parents who did not complete upper secondary education, on average.

Younger adults are more likely to participate in adult education than older adults. The average participation rate among 25-34 year-olds is 62%, while it only reaches 34% among 55-64 year-olds. This is possibly because of older people being outside the workforce, low employer invest-ment in older workers and fewer incentives for older workers to improve their skills.

About 25% of adults are interested in taking part in adult learning but are not able to do so. This varies from more than 33% in Denmark, Korea and the United States, to less than 15% in Poland, the Russian Federation and the Slovak Republic. The two main reasons for not being able to take part are work and family responsibilities.

Professional development for teachers is also important, and is compulsory in 25 of the 33 countries with available data. A lifelong learning approach to teacher development is essential, considering that expectations of staff may change over time. For example, the growing diversity of learners, the greater integration of children and students with special needs, and the increasing use of information and communication technologies all demand that teachers continuously upgrade their skills. High-quality professional development can also help keep teachers in the profession.

Definitions

Adult education refers to formal and/or non-formal education and training. Data on skills are based on the Survey of Adult Skills (PIAAC) 2012. Data on teacher learning are from the 2013 OECD-INES Survey on developing teachers' knowledge and skills and refer to the school year 2012-13.

Information on data for Israel: *http://dx.doi.org/10.1787/888932315602.*

Going further

For additional material, notes and a full explanation of sourcing and methodologies, see *Education at a Glance 2014* (Indicator C6 and D7).

Areas covered include:

- Adult education by age, educational attainment and skill level.
- Professional development for teachers.

Further reading from OECD

OECD (2014), *TALIS 2013 Results: An International Perspective on Teaching and Learning*, OECD Publishing, Paris, *http://dx.doi.org/10.1787/9789264196261-en.*

OECD *Reviews of Vocational Education and Training* (series).

Figure 6.11. **Participation in adult learning, 2012**

This figure shows the percentage 25-64 year-olds who participated in adult education.

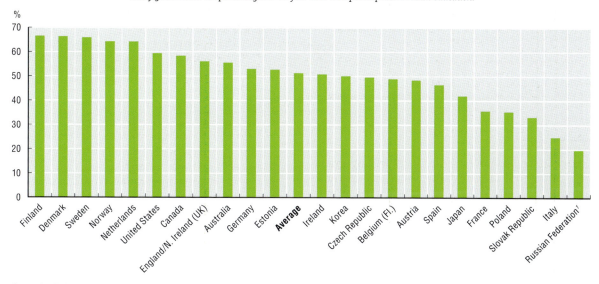

1. Data do not include Moscow municipal area.
Source: OECD (2014), *Education at a Glance 2014*, Chart C6.1, available at *http://dx.doi.org/10.1787/888933119207*.

Figure 6.12. **Participation in adult learning, by parents' level of education, 2012**

This figure shows the percentage of adults with at least one tertiary-educated parent participating in adult education, compared to those with parents who did not complete upper secondary education.

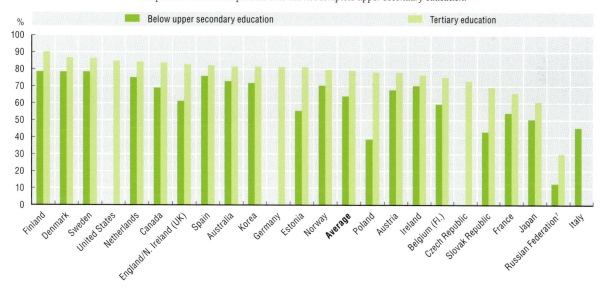

1. Data do not include Moscow municipal area.
Source: OECD (2014), *Education at a Glance 2014*, Chart C6.4, available at *http://dx.doi.org/10.1787/888933119264*.

Statistical note

Coverage of statistics

Although a lack of data still limits the scope of the indicators in many countries, the coverage extends, in principle, to the entire national education system (within the national territory) regardless of the ownership or sponsorship of the institutions concerned and regardless of education delivery mechanisms. With one exception described below, all types of students and all age groups are meant to be included: children (including students with special needs), adults, nationals, foreigners, as well as students in open distance learning, in special education programmes or in educational programmes organised by ministries other than the Ministry of Education, provided the main aim of the programme is the educational development of the individual. However, vocational and technical training in the workplace, with the exception of combined school and work-based programmes that are explicitly deemed to be parts of the education system, is not included in the basic education expenditure and enrolment data.

Educational activities classified as "adult" or "non-regular" are covered, provided that the activities involve studies or have a subject matter content similar to "regular" education studies or that the underlying programmes lead to potential qualifications similar to corresponding regular educational programmes. Courses for adults that are primarily for general interest, personal enrichment, leisure or recreation are excluded.

Calculation of international means

For many indicators an OECD average is presented and for some an OECD total.

OECD average: This is calculated as the unweighted mean of the data values of all OECD countries for which data are available or can be estimated. The OECD average therefore refers to an average of data values at the level of the national systems and can be used to answer the question of how an indicator value for a given country compares with the value for a typical or average country. It does not take into account the absolute size of the education system in each country.

OECD total: This is calculated as a weighted mean of the data values of all OECD countries for which data are available or can be estimated. It reflects the value for a given indicator when the OECD area is considered as a whole. This approach is taken for the purpose of comparing, for example, expenditure charts for individual countries with those of the entire OECD area for which valid data are available, with this area considered as a single entity.

EU21 average: This is calculated as the unweighted mean of the data values of the 21 members of the European Union for which data are available or can be estimated (see the Reader's Guide).

G20 average: This is calculated as the unweighted mean of the data values of all G20 countries (see the Reader's Guide) for which data are available or can be estimated (the European Commission is not included in the calculation). The G20 average is not computed if data for China or India are not available.

Glossary

Adult education: Adult education corresponds to formal and/or non-formal education and training. Formal education and training is defined as planned education provided in the system of schools, colleges, universities and other formal educational institutions, and which normally constitutes a continuous "ladder" of full-time education for children and young people. Non-formal education and training is defined as a sustained educational activity that does not correspond exactly to the above definition of formal education.

Ancillary services: Ancillary services are services provided by educational institutions that are peripheral to the main educational mission. The two main components of ancillary services are student welfare services and services for the general public.

Capital expenditure: Capital expenditure corresponds to education spending on assets that last longer than one year, including construction, renovation or major repair of buildings and new or replacement equipment.

Class size: Class size is the average number of students per class, calculated by dividing the number of students enrolled by the number of classes.

Completion rates: Completion rates are based on the proportion of new entrants into a specified level of education who graduate with at least a first degree at this level in the amount of time normally allocated for completing the programme.

Compulsory education: Compulsory education refers to the legal age from which children are no longer compelled to attend school (*e.g.,* 15th birthday).

Current expenditure: Current expenditure corresponds to education spending on goods and services consumed within the current year, which needs to be made recurrently to sustain the production of educational services.

Educational attainment: Educational attainment is expressed by the highest completed level of education, defined according to the International Standard Classification of Education (ISCED).

Educational personnel: The classification is based on four main functional categories i) Instructional personnel; ii) Professional support for students; iii) Management/Quality control/Administration; and iv) Maintenance and operations personnel. Teaching staff (teachers) and teachers' aides make up the category instructional personnel.

Education expectancy: Education expectancy is the average duration of formal education in which a five-year-old child can expect to enroll over his or her lifetime.

Employment rate: Employment rates represent the number of persons in employment as a percentage of the working-age population. The employed are defined as those who work for pay or profit for at least one hour a week, or who have a job but are temporarily not at work due to illness, leave or industrial action.

Enrolment rates: Enrolment rates represent the number of students of a particular age group enrolled in all levels of education as a percentage of the total population of that age group.

Expenditure on educational core services: Expenditure on educational core services includes all expenditure that is directly related to instruction and education. This should cover all expenditure on teachers, school buildings, teaching materials, books, tuition outside schools and administration of schools.

Foreign students: Foreign students are students who do not hold the citizenship of the country for which the data are collected.

Full-time worker: Full-time workers work usually 30 hours or more on their main job.

General programmes: General programmes are programmes that are not designed explicitly to prepare participants for a specific class of occupations or trades or for entry into further vocational or technical education programmes.

Gross Domestic Product (GDP): Gross Domestic Product (GDP) is the standard measure of the value of final goods and services produced by a country during a period minus the value of imports.

Human capital: Human capital is productive wealth embodied in labour, skills and knowledge.

Intended instruction time: Intended instruction time refers to the number of hours per year for which students ought to receive instruction in both the compulsory and non-compulsory parts of the curriculum.

International students: International students are students who left their country of origin and moved to another country to study.

Lower secondary education: Lower secondary education completes the provision of basic education, usually in a more subject-oriented way with more specialist teachers. Entry follows 6 years of primary education; duration is 3 years. In some countries, the end of this level marks the end of compulsory education.

Net graduation rates: Net graduation rates refer to the estimated percentage of people from a specific age group who will complete tertiary education over their lifetimes, based on current patterns of graduation.

PISA or Programme for International Student Assessment: The Programme for International Student Assessment is an international study conducted by the OECD which measures how well young adults, at age 15 and therefore approaching the end of compulsory schooling, are prepared to meet the challenges of today's knowledge societies.

Post-secondary non-tertiary level of education: Programmes at this level may be regarded nationally as part of upper secondary or post-secondary education, but in terms of international comparison their status is less clear cut. Programme content may not be much more advanced than in upper secondary, and is certainly lower than at tertiary level. Entry typically requires completion of an upper secondary programme. Duration is usually equivalent to between 6 months and 2 years of full-time study.

Pre-primary education: Pre-primary education is the first stage of organised instruction designed to introduce very young children to the school atmosphere (minimum entry age of 3).

Primary education: Primary education is designed to provide a sound basic education in reading, writing and mathematics and a basic understanding of some other subjects (entry age: between 5 and 7). Duration is of 6 years.

Private expenditure: Private expenditure refers to expenditure funded by private sources, i.e. households and other private entities. "Households" refers to students and their families. "Other private entities" include private business firms and non-profit organisations, including religious organisations, charitable organisations, and business and labour associations.

Private institution: An institution is classified as private if it is controlled and managed by a nongovernmental organisation (e.g., a Church, Trade Union or business enterprise), or if its Governing Board consists mostly of members not selected by a public agency.

Private internal rate of return: The rate of return represents a measure of the returns obtained, over time, relative to the costs of the initial investment in education.

Public institution: An institution is classified as public if it is controlled and managed directly by a public education authority or agency; or is controlled and managed either by a government agency directly or by a governing body (Council, Committee etc.), most of whose members are appointed by a public authority or elected by public franchise.

Relative earnings: Relative earnings are percentages of the earnings of adults with levels of education other than upper secondary relative to the earnings of those with upper secondary education.

Statutory teaching time: Statutory teaching time is defined as the scheduled number of 60-minute hours per year that a full-time teacher teaches a group or class of students as set by policy.

Survey of Adult Skills (PIAAC): The Survey of Adult Skills, a product of the OECD Programme for the International Assessment of Adult Competencies (PIAAC), is an international study conducted by the OECD that assesses the proficiency of adults from age 16 onwards in literacy, numeracy and problem solving in technology-rich environments. These skills are "key information-processing competencies" that are relevant to adults in many social contexts and work situations, and necessary for fully integrating and participating in the labour market, education and training, and social and civic life.

Unemployment rate: Unemployment rates represent the number of unemployed persons as a percentage of the labour force. The unemployed are defined as people without work but actively seeking employment and currently available to start work.

University-level education: "Long-stream" programmes that are theory based and aimed at preparing students for further research or to give access to highly skilled professions, such as medicine or architecture. Entry preceded by 13 years of education and students are typically required to have completed upper secondary or post-secondary non-tertiary education. Duration equivalent to at least 3 years of full-time study, but 4 is more usual.

Upper secondary education: Upper secondary education corresponds to the final stage of secondary education in most OECD countries. Even stronger subject specialisation than at lower-secondary level, with teachers usually more qualified. Students are typically expected to have completed 9 years of education or lower secondary schooling before entry and are generally around the age of 15 or 16.

Vocationally oriented tertiary education: "Short-stream" programmes that are more practically oriented or focus on the skills needed for students to directly enter specific occupations. Entry is preceded by 13 years of education; duration equivalent to at least 2 years of full-time study, but 3 is more usual.

Vocational programmes: Vocational education prepares participants for direct entry, without further training, into specific occupations. Successful completion of such programmes leads to a labour-market relevant vocational qualification.

Working time (for teachers): Working time refers to the number of hours that a full-time teacher is expected to work. According to a country's formal policy, it can refer to time directly associated with teaching as well as the hours devoted to teaching-related activities, such as preparing lessons, counselling students, correcting assignments and tests, and meeting with parents and other staff.

Further reading

PISA

Launched in 1997 by the OECD, the Programme for International Student Assessment (PISA) is an international study which aims to evaluate education systems worldwide by testing the skills and knowledge of 15-year-old students. To date, students representing more than 70 countries and economies have participated in the assessment.

In 2000 the focus of the assessment was reading, in 2003 mathematics and problem solving, in 2006 science and in 2009 reading again. The 2012 data collection focussed on mathematics, and included an optional computer-based assessment of mathematics and reading involving some 30 countries as well as an optional area of assessment: financial literacy, which 19 countries took up. The 2012 results are compiled into 6 volumes:

What Students Know and Can Do (Volume I), http://dx.doi.org/10.1787/9789264208780-en.

Excellence through Equity (Volume II), http://dx.doi.org/10.1787/9789264201132-en.

Ready to Learn (Volume III), http://dx.doi.org/10.1787/9789264201170-en.

What Makes Schools Successful (Volume IV), http://dx.doi.org/10.1787/9789264201156-en.

Creative Problem Solving (Volume V), http://dx.doi.org/10.1787/9789264208070-en.

Students and Money (Volume VI), http://dx.doi.org/10.1787/9789264208094-en.

Equity, Excellence and Inclusiveness in Education

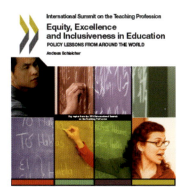

Excellence in education without equity risks leading to large economic and social disparities; equity in education at the expense of quality is a meaningless aspiration. This book identifies some of the steps policy makers can take to build school systems that are both equitable and excellent, and provides examples that illustrate proven or promising practices in specific countries.

http://dx.doi.org/10.1787/9789264214033-en.

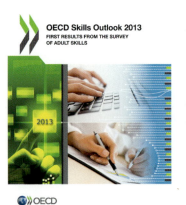

OECD Reviews of Vocational Education and Training

Higher level vocational education and training (VET) programmes, known as career and technical education in the United States, are facing rapid change and intensifying challenges. What type of training is needed to meet the needs of changing economies? How should the programmes be funded? How should they be linked to academic and university programmes? How can employers and unions be engaged? The country reports in this series look at these and other questions. They form part of Skills beyond School, the OECD policy review of postsecondary vocational education and training.

http://dx.doi.org/10.1787/20777736.

OECD Skills Outlook 2013

This book presents the initial results of the Survey of Adult Skills (PIAAC), which evaluates the skills of adults in 22 OECD member countries and two partner countries. It examines the social and economic context, the supply of key information processing skills, who has these skills at what level, the supply of and demand for these skills in the labour market, the acquisition and maintenance of skills over a lifetime, and how proficiency in these skills translates into better economic and social outcomes.

http://dx.doi.org/10.1787/9789264204256-en.

Education at a Glance country-specific material:

Country notes with key fact tables and **multilingual summaries** for 34 OECD member countries, 8 non-OECD member countries, as well as the European Union.

Financial Education for Youth: The Role of Schools (2014), http://dx.doi.org/10.1787/9789264174825-en.

TALIS 2013 Results: An International Perspective on Teaching and Learning (2014), http://dx.doi.org/10.1787/9789264196261-en.

OECD Factbook (2014), http://dx.doi.org/10.1787/factbook-2014-en.

Society at a Glance 2014: OECD Social Indicators (2014), http://dx.doi.org/10.1787/soc_glance-2014-en.

Leadership for 21st Century Learning (2013), http://dx.doi.org/10.1787/9789264205406-en.

Women and Financial Education: Evidence, Policy Responses and Guidance (2013), http://dx.doi.org/10.1787/9789264202733-en.

Innovative Learning Environments (2013), http://dx.doi.org/10.1787/9789264203488-en.

Education Today 2013: The OECD Perspective (2013), http://dx.doi.org/10.1787/edu_today-2013-en.

Trends Shaping Education 2013 (2013), http://dx.doi.org/10.1787/trends_edu-2013-en.

Better Skills, Better Jobs, Better Lives: A Strategic Approach to Skills Policies (2013), http://dx.doi.org/10.1787/9789264177338-en.

Art for Art's Sake?: The Impact of Arts Education (2013), http://dx.doi.org/10.1787/9789264180789-en.

Teachers for the 21st Century: Using Evaluation to Improve Teaching (2013), http://dx.doi.org/10.1787/9789264193864-en.

PISA 2012 Assessment and Analytical Framework : Mathematics, Reading, Science, Problem Solving and Financial Literacy (2013), http://dx.doi.org/10.1787/9789264190511-en.

Health at a Glance 2013: OECD Indicators (2013), http://dx.doi.org/10.1787/health_glance-2013-en.

Equity and Quality in Education: Supporting Disadvantaged Students and Schools (2012), http://dx.doi.org/10.1787/9789264130852-en.

How's Life?2013: Measuring Well-being (2013), http://dx.doi.org/10.1787/9789264201392-en.

ORGANISATION FOR ECONOMIC CO-OPERATION AND DEVELOPMENT

The OECD is a unique forum where governments work together to address the economic, social and environmental challenges of globalisation. The OECD is also at the forefront of efforts to understand and to help governments respond to new developments and concerns, such as corporate governance, the information economy and the challenges of an ageing population. The Organisation provides a setting where governments can compare policy experiences, seek answers to common problems, identify good practice and work to co-ordinate domestic and international policies.

The OECD member countries are: Australia, Austria, Belgium, Canada, Chile, the Czech Republic, Denmark, Estonia, Finland, France, Germany, Greece, Hungary, Iceland, Ireland, Israel, Italy, Japan, Korea, Luxembourg, Mexico, the Netherlands, New Zealand, Norway, Poland, Portugal, the Slovak Republic, Slovenia, Spain, Sweden, Switzerland, Turkey, the United Kingdom and the United States. The European Union takes part in the work of the OECD.

OECD Publishing disseminates widely the results of the Organisation's statistics gathering and research on economic, social and environmental issues, as well as the conventions, guidelines and standards agreed by its members.

OECD PUBLISHING, 2, rue André-Pascal, 75775 PARIS CEDEX 16
(96 2014 03 1 P) ISBN 978-92-64-21501-6 – 2014-02